BOURNE TO RALLY
POSSUM BOURNE

THE AUTOBIOGRAPHY

ACKNOWLEDGEMENTS

Part of the proceeds from the sale of this book are being donated to the Possum Bourne Family Trust.

Grant Sheehan of Phantom House Books thanks the following people and companies for their input and assistance:

Paul Owen, Natalie Gray, Shelley-Maree Cassidy, Murray Brown, Moya Rhodes, Oliver Midgley, Glenn Mettam and Harbour City Motor Company (Wellington), John Coker and Subaru New Zealand.

Special thanks to Possum's wife Peggy, his mother Peggy, his sister Kristine Game, and all of his family, friends and colleagues who gave their time to help tell Possum's story.

All photographs are from the Bourne family's collection, unless otherwise credited. Efforts to trace the photographers of some of the shots prior to publication have been unsuccessful, so the publisher and the Bourne family thank those who recorded Possum's exploits over many years.

Edited by Chris Ryan
Designed by Typeface Limited
Printed in Hongkong by Toppan Printing Co (HK) Ltd

First published in New Zealand in 2003 by Phantom House Books Ltd
Reprinted 2003
P.O. Box 6385 Marion Square
Wellington
New Zealand
Email info@phantomhouse.com
www.phantomhouse.com

ISBN 0-9582388-1-2

BOURNE TO RALLY
POSSUM BOURNE

THE AUTOBIOGRAPHY

WITH

PAUL OWEN

PHANTOM HOUSE

CONTENTS

FOREWORD

The first time I met Possum Bourne face to face in 1998, he was totally in his element, sitting at the wheel of an ex-works Group A Subaru rallycar. I strapped myself into the right-side passenger's seat, and Possum introduced himself with a beaming smile and a handshake. He then went on to scare the cholesterol out of me by chucking the Impreza sideways at 200 km/h, and drifting it to within millimetres of the rather large gum trees that lined that particular stage of the Canberra Rally. The wicked grin on Possum's face suggested he really enjoyed his job. Unlike just about every other motorsport professional, Possum really relished PR work. As a man of the people, with one of the most positive attitudes on the planet, Possum had the right stuff to become "the face of Subaru" in down under markets. No car company ever had a more passionate or a more enthusiastic ambassador for the brand.

The first time I really got to know Possum was at the start of 2003, when we started working on this book together. Few writers are as fortunate with their subject matter. Few get to weave a life's tapestry from such richly coloured threads of information. Possum might have missed scoring a half-century in the number of years he was with us, but in terms of what he did and achieved with his time, he lived a long and satisfying life.

Possum gave himself quite a schedule for 2003. He finally achieved his long cherished dream of competing in the World Rally Championship. This, coupled with his commitment to the Australian Rally Championship, made him the busiest rally driver of the season. The logistics involved with moving three rally cars around the globe, and finding the time to do the lengthy recces and testing that being competitive in a rally requires, placed more demands on Possum's time than ever. Yet, his enthusiasm for the book never waned. While it didn't have top priority, Possum found time whenever he could so that we could get together and record more transcripts. I didn't know then just how precious this time was.

Through working with Possum I got to meet his family and friends. The two Peggys in his life – his Mum, and his wife – were vital supporters at crucial moments in his career. Possum was a lucky man in the love and support he received at home. His youngest sister Kristine became his keeper, a personal assistant who could make some sense out of the chaos of his schedule. Possum Bourne Motorsport attracted a team of dedicated people from manager Murray Brown down. Yet, it was more than luck that drew the right people to him. It was respect as well. No one wanted Possum to win more than those who worked for him, and those who loved and supported him.

The last time I saw Possum Bourne, he was sitting in his kitchen with his three-year old daughter, Jazlin, on his knee. It was the Wednesday before that fateful Friday, and we'd just conducted our final interview for the book. The family was getting ready to go to Queenstown, and Peggy had gone out to tie up the loose ends. During that afternoon I saw another side of Possum – the father of three young children. In Peggy's absence, the kids were competing with each other for his attention, yet he was patient, quietly-spoken, and firm in his discipline of them. This is how I'll remember him most – not as New Zealand's first and only resident FIA rally champion – but for his greater achievements as a Dad.

Possum had a great talent for being able to see the positive side of any personal disappointment or setback. So how do the people he leaves behind find anything positive in his tragic and sudden death? We find it in the example he set for all of us. Possum overcame huge odds and an obvious geographical handicap to become a "colonial" factory rally driver in a sport where the best seats are usually reserved for Europeans. And, he did that mostly on the strength of his positive attitude, and sheer determination to succeed no matter what.

Paul Owen
April 30, 2003

CHAPTER ONE

THE DREAM COMES TRUE

It's the most important meeting of my career, and I'm late. Whirlpools of traffic around London's ring roads threaten to suck my dream to be a works rally driver under, and any gap in the gridlock is quickly closed with a quick downshift or two for a burst of speed. I wonder what I should say if I'm pulled over? "Sorry officer, I know I'm speeding, but I'm late to sign a major deal to drive a factory Subaru rally car" would be telling the truth. But the likely response from the officer in this part of the world is that I don't look or sound like Colin McRae; nor Ari Vatanen, for that matter. And, after further enquiries: "What kind of a name is Possum anyway?"

I'm really just another traveller caught in London's web of traffic at this stage in my driving career. It's December 1992, and although "Possum Bourne" may be a driver a few will instantly recognise in the rally world, I'm not yet the household name I hope to become in the Asia-Pacific region. But I have worked hard and built up some great relationships and friends in my chosen sport of rallying that are now opening doors for me.

It was a call from PR Plus, a Hong Kong-based promotions company, that changed my life. PR Plus director Walter Ngah rang me and said, "We've got these people who are really keen on the Hong Kong-Beijing rally, and they're looking for a driver who can do a good job, so we thought of you."

Their client turned out to be the British American Tobacco Company (BAT). It would lead to the formation of a Subaru and Prodrive-run "super team" backed by BAT and it would mean a big jump forward in my career.

Several long-distance phone calls later, plus Prodrive and Subaru Tecnica International joining the project, and I'm on my way to sign for a team destined to dominate rallying in the mid-1990s. It's the first time that my long-held dream of becoming a factory rally driver has looked like becoming a reality. When I started rallying, I never imagined I'd come this far. Sure, I'd always thought it would be nice to have that level of support, but you've got to be realistic about what you can achieve, otherwise you just become frustrated at your lack of progress. I couldn't ever see how I could go from the New Zealand national championship to driving in the World Championship. That's way too big a step for anyone to contemplate, no matter how good they think they are. So the idea was to build a path of many steps to that goal. Rallying is no different to any other sport or business. You've got to sit down, put it all together, and make it into some sort of achievable package. Set goals that are achievable, and you make it possible to turn the dream into reality. The big thing to remember is it's not what you know, it's who you know that will help the most.

Yet it all feels surreal as we speed through the London traffic, burn up the M40 and M25 at over 100 mph, and take the next exit after Heathrow towards BAT's headquarters in Staines. I'm so close to achieving my dream, and I'm freaking out about being late. For relationships are as important in sport as in any other part of life. One of the rules I live my life by is "never burn a bridge", and it's serving me well here. I first got to know Walter from the days he used to come down to New Zealand to compete in rallies himself. I gave him a hand, and it sparked a friendship. You just help people out; in this sport it's the way it is. Relationships are built from the smallest possible beginnings. People often forget that.

Same thing with Subaru. By this time, I've been driving the boxer-engine cars for a decade, and the President of Subaru Tecnica International, Mr Kuze, treats me almost like a son. He's a tough mentor, but fair and always straight. If it weren't for Mr Kuze, I wouldn't be driving down this road to Staines right now towards the deal of my career. Nearly all my international drives up until this point have been as a result of his support, and I suspect he's as much a driver of the proposed team structure as David Richards, Managing Director of Prodrive. It was Mr Kuze who persuaded Prodrive to support me in one of their cars for the 1992 Rally of New Zealand. By putting me in their machinery, they gained an accurate impression of the skills I felt I could bring to their team. When I had a great first day and then started catching rally leader Carlos Sainz in his factory Toyota on the second leg, it gave me plenty of credibility in the eyes of Dave Richards.

We had some great stage times on my home turf of the Maramarua Forest, then lost the engine in a year where we always seemed to be having mechanical problems. That was one of the many birth pains for the team before the coming of the Subaru 555 World Rally team; but essentially it was their car, so it gave a great impression of how competitive a Kiwi enclave within the Prodrive team structure could be.

The mission I've decided to accept is to try to win the FIA Asia-Pacific Rally Championship for the Subaru 555 World Rally team for three years in a row – 1993, 1994, and 1995. I'm to be first reserve for the FIA World Rally Championship rounds if anything happens to either Colin McRae or Ari Vatanen, and they'll help me out in the FIA Asia Pacific Rally Championship rounds that suit their schedule. For three rallies of the 1993 season – Hong Kong-Beijing, Australia, and New Zealand – the team will run three cars in a show of strength unrivalled by any other factory team. The deal will double the budget I'm normally used to working with.

It usually costs around $600,000 to run in the Australian or New Zealand championships, with occasional international events thrown in for good measure. And that's not counting the cost of the machinery. Becoming BAT-sponsored will give the team between three and four million pounds to run two cars in the APRC rounds. That also means I will get a proper driving fee.

It's not moonbeams money by any means, but it sure beats working nine to five. Peggy, my wife, is as excited as hell about it. She's been through the tough bits, seen me spend just about every cent we've had on getting to the start-line, and now, there's finally a crack at making a reasonable wage at it.

Rodger Freeth, my co-driver, is equally thrilled. He's been a New Zealand motorsport identity for years – a multi-winner of national motorcycle racing titles, a talented circuit racer in his Toyota Starlet V8, and someone about to become the New Zealand land speed record holder. Yet he's never made any money at it, and motorsport is something he's always fitted around his day-job of lecturing in mathematics and astrophysics at Auckland University.

So at last a bunch of Kiwis are to be included in the highest
level of the sport I love – me, Rodger, and the group of trusted
friends that have helped me through the years are also in my
support crew. That's the best part for me. I don't have a manager,
but I've got the guys I trust most to work on my car included in
the deal. Perhaps negotiating the driving fee was the hardest
part, for it's always tough to sell yourself and put a price on
your talent. But when it came to the team structure, I knew
exactly what I wanted – a bunch of guys prepared to cut their
right arms off for me and watch my back if required. Guys like
Kevin Sanderson, Chris Kitzen, Ray Swain, Wayne Rogers and
Steve Cribb. Steve is our logistics guy, and can work like a ferret.
He can sniff out sources of parts, and cut through red tape with
a hot machete. He would prove vital in the coming season, as
Rodger and I really don't know what we are getting ourselves
into yet. We've rallied in Malaysia before, but the rest of Asia
might as well have been located on another planet.

Pulling into BAT's headquarters this December day is therefore
a journey into the unknown. I'm used to running my own team,
making the calls, and now I'm about to become a hired gun.
Moving up to this more professional level makes rallying
something I no longer do purely for fun and enjoyment. There's
a lot more responsibility landing on my shoulders, given the
huge budget that BAT are injecting into the team and my bid to

be Asia-Pacific champion. I walk into BAT's offices with mixed emotions. There's a feeling that I've finally "arrived" in more ways than just beating the London traffic. But there's also the sense that rallying is about to change for me, that it is about to become much more a business than a sport. It's always been important to me that people like me, that they see me as a friend rather than anything else. Now I'm about to place myself in a position that others in the sport will envy, and need to watch my back more closely.

Ari and Colin are already there, waiting to put their signatures on contracts that would bring the 555 Subaru world rally team to life. Ari, who I already know well, a man you can't help but like, is the first person I talk to. He's one of the nicest people I've ever met, a very religious man with a fantastic philosophy on life. If you are feeling down, a talk with Ari always picks you up. I've learnt a lot from him about how to deal with the PR side of the rallying contract. A press conference with Ari is always an entertaining event. He answers questions with such detail and humour, the press just hang on every word. In Indonesia he'd prove that, even when we're all drowning in the depths of shit and mud, he could still be positive. My friend from Kenya, Mike Kirkland, once joked that Ari would be president of Finland one day. In 1999 he would become a member of the European parliament.

Colin would take just a little longer for me to get to know, but not much. Like Ari, he would become a friend for life, the bonds made stronger in the coming campaign together. Rallying is like no other motorsport in that you spend a lot of time with the other drivers in your team, sorting the cars and the pace notes for the coming event. There's more opportunity to view the other drivers in the team as working for you and the team, than against you, unlike the more cut-throat world of circuit racing.

The three of us make a formidable trio of drivers – Ari the wily veteran, Colin the rapidly-rising star, and me: someone who'd shown what I thought was plenty of potential, finally getting the break I'd worked hard for. After we sign the contracts, BAT bring out the cocktails to celebrate and we meet the people we are going to work closely with. That evening, from my hotel, I ring Rodger in New Zealand.

"The job's done, the deal's signed, and we're in."

He lets out a cheer of delight.

"You know, I've always wanted to make motorsport my real living," he replies, "Now it looks like it's finally going to happen."

We weren't about to make a huge amount of money, but we were on the right road. I felt we were finally getting somewhere, and could now afford to sort out some areas that were never priorities before – such as getting proper insurance cover for our families and us if anything went horribly wrong.

Next day I drive to Prodrive's headquarters in Banbury to start sorting the cars. Part of the delivery test includes choosing the colour scheme for the team. There are cars of various colour combinations, and we drive them on a Silverstone forest stage to see how they'll look on television. There are cream-coloured cars, yellow cars, and others, but the one that really stands out on the replays is the brilliant blue with simple yellow lettering. It really is eye-catching, and delivers the sponsor's logo loud and clear. Once all the mechanics and service vehicles are decked out in the same colours, the 555 Subaru World rally team will stand out from the rest. Such visual impact makes the whole promotional thing that much easier, and images of these cars would go on to grace the covers of magazines, computer games and posters on bedroom walls the world over.

It's tough coming into an English team. There's a different mentality in the Prodrive "camp" than the atmosphere I'm used to. I find them very conservative, almost cold, and not very communicative. I'm used to knowing everything that's going on with my car, but it's the opposite here. You really have to dig to find out what is going on. I try to break the ice, try to get the respect of the Poms I haven't met before. That's my biggest challenge as a down-to-earth bloke from Pukekohe, a market gardening town south of Auckland. Respect for the driver is vital, because that's what motivates a support crew to go the extra distance for you. They'll always do a professional job at this level, but going the extra step requires respect. If you haven't got it at the work face, then you're stuffed as a driver. Getting them working hard for you takes care of everything. I wanted to move to England to be close to Banbury, and the development of the cars. I saw that as a necessary step to keeping on top of things, and keeping some control of my destiny, but Prodrive didn't want me to base myself there. Perhaps they see my involvement as a short-term step, and have earmarked me to be a regional star at best. I don't think it's got anything to do with my nationality - my "down-under" origins – because I believe that you can turn yourself into the right PR tool no matter where you're from. Former New Zealand rally champion Paul Adams once gave me good advice on how to deal with the press:

"It doesn't matter what's happened," he said. "Make sure you have a story, and it's the truth. Don't bullshit, and the media will be good to you." Like Ari, he's another rally driver now turned politician.

Helping out with PR was how I saw myself best fitting in at Banbury, because as a New Zealander, I couldn't bring in any extra sponsorship money to help make the whole 555 Subaru thing work. Colin didn't like the PR side of the job much, and I thought it's one of my strengths, maybe I can help shoulder his load.

So, my offer to move declined, I head back home to start one of the busiest seasons of my career.

Rodger and I don't really know if we've bitten off more than we can chew. Squeezing in the Asia-Pacific rounds with our commitments for the Australian title will mean contesting nine events over a seven-month period of 1993. There's a great deal of logistics to get into place. When I visit Rodger on my return to New Zealand, he gets out his new world atlas CD and loads it into his computer.

We look up Indonesia, where the first round of the Asia-Pacific Championship will be held. This is the first time I've ever taken an interest in the country with the fourth largest population in the world. According to the CD, it's full of rubber trees, palm oil plantations, and rice paddies. And people – millions and millions of them. There's no mention of the state of the roads.

Nothing really prepared us for our arrival in Medan, Sumatra, in June 1993. Medan is a rough-as-guts place, and the hotel is even rougher. The ambient air temperature is 46℃, and the inside of the Legacy is like a blast furnace. Practising, we can't believe the change in road conditions that happens with the afternoon rains. One minute the hard-packed dirt peels rubber off our tyres at the braking points, leaving black lines on the surface; the next it's as soft as cottonwool. It rains that hard. Harder than I've ever seen in New Zealand: a country more prone to flood than drought. Here in Medan you can't even stand up on a gentle slope. We had a parked truck slide into a ditch during one of those afternoon showers. The rain just washed away the dirt beneath the tyres and took the truck with it. It was unbelievable.

We start practising around a block full of the 90-degree corners that are typical of Indonesian roads; Ari and I taking the engineers for a ride so we can dial in the cars. Entering the last corner of the course, the rain starts hammering down, and suddenly takes all the traction away. The back of the car goes in and out and every which way, but we get away with it. Ari isn't so lucky. He just goes straight off and clips the trees with the back guard. He gets back onto the road, but second time around, does the same thing big time, and knocks the car around a little. Welcome to Indonesia! The engineers call an end to the test, saying, "It's time to go home, because we don't want the cars wrecked."

Maybe they just want to get somewhere dry. There had been rivers of water running off their noses as they bent over and worked on the cars. Everyone had already been as sick as a dog because they weren't used to the spicy food, and the local water was undrinkable. The whole scene lacked the glamour associated with events like the Monte Carlo Rally.

Yet the team photo taken before the start of the event has all the appearance of a professional well-funded factory rally team. I'm standing by my car with Rodger, Ari and Bruno Burglund (Ari's co-driver), flanked by our crews in their matching blue team kit. As the flashbulbs pop, it starts to sink in that I'm a factory driver for Subaru. I'm standing next to the great Ari Vatanen, the man the press call the "Flying Finn". Fourteen or so years before I was driving the milk tanker as fast as I could safely go, finishing my round early so I could go and watch Ari hammer his BDA Escort through the pine trees in the Rally of New Zealand. He inspired me to go rallying that day; now I'm standing here next to him as his team-mate. And I'm actually the lead driver for this event. He's here to help me out. This is something a young Pukekohe mechanic and truck driver could scarcely have dreamed of fourteen years ago. I glance at Rodger in disbelief.

However, the events of 1993 would teach me that while even the most fantastic of dreams can come true, there's always a catch. And so began the season that would be both the best, and the worst, of my life.

THE BEGINNING OF PETER RAYMOND GEORGE BOURNE

If you told me that I'd become a works rally driver when I was a kid growing up on a farm south of Auckland, I'd never have believed you. Anyone who asked me what I wanted to be in those days got a quick response: truck driver. I was mad about the things. We had a dairy farm, on Springhills Road, just south of the Meremere township, and every year I'd look forward to the hay season, because it was a chance to get behind the wheel. As a kid, I'd drive the truck picking up the hay, or lap the paddocks with the tractor cutting the grass in ever-decreasing circles. It was the highlight of my childhood.

I was the quiet, shy, second kid of five born to Ray and Peggy Bourne. I arrived on a Black Friday at Pukekohe Hospital in 1956 to be followed two years later by my brother Geoffrey, then my sisters Deb and Kristine at similar intervals. Neville, the brother that preceded me by two years, I never got to know. When I was six months old, and Neville was nearing his third birthday, he accidentally fell into a container of boiling water in the milk shed, and died ten days later. It was a tragedy that would have driven many marriages to destruction, but the bonds

between Mum and Dad were stronger than rawhide. She got her fun-loving nature from growing up in a large family of ten kids, while Dad had to grow up early to take over the day-to-day running of the farm from his elderly parents. The only break he got from the farm was when he joined the J-force that occupied Japan immediately after World War Two. His parents gave him just ten shillings a week for all his work, precious funds he spent on taking Mum to the pictures when they were courting. They had met at a homecoming dance held in his honour at the Meremere hall when he returned from Japan.

Meremere was the nearest village for farms in our area. It was a town that had sprung up virtually overnight with the building of a coal-fired power station by the banks of the Waikato River. A primary school was part of the power station complex, and we went there. Not that I had much interest in school. I didn't like reading much, maths had some appeal, but most of the time I couldn't wait to get back home to the rhythms and routines of farm life.

Dad had left school when he was 12, and had started running the family farm from age 13. Like most people of his era, the Great Depression of the 1930s, and World War Two, had left their influence on him. He constantly worried about money, and every resource on the farm was carefully looked after. Nothing was wasted, and he kept anything that might come in handy some day. In later years, when I started getting involved in motorsport, it was hard for him to understand why I was heading down that road. He couldn't see any financial gain in it, and couldn't grasp the idea of competing in a highly expensive sport just for the fun of it all. Looking back, it's easy to see how some of his attitudes rubbed off on me. I'm pretty tight with team funds, and very careful where I spend them. Dad's motto was "why spend two shillings if you can get away with one?"

He also taught me that a job is only worth doing if it's done right. This gave me quite a conservative approach to my rallying. In the beginning, I'd only compete if there were enough resources to do the job properly, such as having enough tyres to get a result. If there weren't enough, I simply wouldn't enter, and would save what I had for the next event.

Mum grew up in Pokeno, a town to the north of Meremere. Mercer, the town between Pokeno and Meremere, was the place she'd shop so she could keep in touch with the gossip and social life of her hometown. We got our groceries at Calder's Four Square, and the nearest post office and tennis courts were there. Dad's parents used to own the Mercer pub and billiard hall, so that community was like the roots of our family. Most of Mum and Dad's friends lived there. Mum was heavily involved in the community through the Women's Division of Federated Farmers, and the tennis club. She encouraged us to play sport, although Geoffrey was always far better at it than me.

The picture theatre in Meremere did good business in those pre-TV days. Dad used to take us there every Saturday night. There would be newsreels before the main features, but I remember the early James Bond movies most. I thought *Thunderball* was the coolest movie ever made.

Each day, Geoffrey and I would take the cream cans down to the gate for collection. It was my first experience of controlling a motor vehicle, and I'd take care not spill the cream on the bumpy, twisty driveway. It was a 400-metre drive from the milking shed to the gate, but it was steep, and there was a big, sharp turn at the bottom. Dad made it clear to us that spilling the cream wasn't an option. Those three cans of cream would be worth about $3000 in today's money. The collection stand at the gate was higher than the tractor hydraulics would go, so Geoffrey and I would have to lift the cans onto it. They were as heavy as hell, but we'd gladly put in the effort – just for the chance to drive the tractor.

Whenever it was Christmas or my birthday, my collection of Matchbox and Dinky toy cars and trucks would expand. These were my treasures, and I've still got every one of them and the boxes they came in. The model trucks were my favourites, and when I heard my cousin's friend's Dad, Norm Turner, was going to England, I asked him to get me an articulated truck Matchbox toy that I'd seen in a brochure.

I may have been shy, but I wasn't afraid to ask for the things I really wanted – such as wanting to go to the nearby Pukekohe race circuit to watch Bruce McLaren race his Cooper-Climax in the New Zealand Grand Prix. McLaren was my hero in those early years, and, at age seven, I showed up for a fancy dress ball at the Mercer Hall dressed as a racing driver, with my blue pyjamas as a race suit, and McLaren's name and the number seven stitched across my back. Mum covered them with stickers from Sutherland's garage, borrowed a motorcycle helmet, and I wore my gumboots as racing shoes.

The outfit won a prize for best costume but I never got to watch McLaren race, despite pestering Dad to take us to the nearby

New Zealand Grand Prix. He just couldn't see the point in a bunch of blokes burning petrol and tyres to go round and round the same circuit – even when it was Chris Amon in a red Ferrari, battling Jim Clark in a Lotus.

Dad had other things on his mind. Mum got pretty crook for a while there, and had a long stay in hospital. She developed a cyst on her lung, and was laid up for three months. We four kids went to Uncle Jim Wood's farm during the week to ease the burden, returning home at the weekends to help with the milking on the days when there wasn't any school. As the eldest, I had to get the tea on and look after the younger kids while Dad worked.

How I longed for those days when there wasn't any school. I just couldn't wait to get out of the place, especially when Meremere Primary became Pukekohe High School. Starting there meant a 45-minute slog each way on a stinking hot school bus. Willy McGrath and I would always sit up front so we could truck-spot on the way, competing with each other to be first to correctly count the number of axles and tyres. It was anything to break the boredom, for the trip from Meremere to Pukekohe and back seemed to take all day. We'd cheer when the bus broke down on the rough gravel roads because it meant less time at school, and the tired old bus would break down about five or six times a year.

On the holidays, I'd ask Mum's younger brother, Uncle Graham, if I could ride in his cattle truck with him. He worked for Peter Hale Transport, and it was a big treat to drive around with him all day, moving herds with a prime mover. I was hooked on trucks, and thought they would be my life. Even today, I still get a kick out of delivering the rally car somewhere, a sense of satisfaction at driving as part of the economy. One of my schoolmates went on to own Te Kauwhata Transport, and I'd like to think that's what I'd be doing today if motorsport hadn't lured me away.

A wide range of cultures and races attended Pukekohe High School. The school was as diverse as the economy that surrounded it. There were kids whose parents were market gardeners, others whose folks were involved in the horse industry, transport, machinery, dairying, and in back section sheds and small factories in the outer suburbs: motorsport. The community was a melting pot of hard work and respect. As the town grew, so did its horizons. These days it's on Auckland's lifestyle fringe and full of mod cons like supermarkets, cafés, and restaurants.

Back then, there was nothing to do. I couldn't wait to turn 15, the age I could leave school. The age I could get my licence. Dad first taught me to drive in the paddocks of the farm, and Mum had been letting me drive home from Pukekohe ever since I turned 13. By then, I'd served an apprenticeship of sorts, backing the car in and out of the garage, and manoeuvring it around the driveway. The first time I overtook another car with the family station wagon was a rite-of-passage moment I'll never forget. It was on a long straight between Tuakau and Pokeno, and I remember thinking "cracker job, I didn't stuff that up". It was quite nerve-racking giving the station wagon full throttle with Mum sitting alongside in the passenger seat.

I couldn't have been more ready for my licence by the time I reached the age of no-more-dusty-school-buses, and flew straight through my driving test. And straight out the school gates for the last time.

I left school as soon as I could, and became an apprentice at Howe and Weston's garage. They took on three new apprentices a year in those days, for the government of the day knew the importance of fostering trade skills. Towards the end of my fifth form year, I'd pestered Howe and Weston to become one of their three new apprentices. In the end I wore them down. The manager said that if persistence was a measure of my worth, then I was the best apprentice they'd ever taken on. He also said that if my School Certificate results didn't include passes in the subjects related to the job that I'd be shown the door. It was a great relief later in the year when I rang Mum on the day the results arrived in the mail and found I'd passed.

So I walked out of school after three years of secondary education, straight into a job in those days of full employment in New Zealand. Geoffrey and Deb would keep the academic record of the Bourne family straight by going on to university, and Kristine would bring her organising and management skills to help my efforts, as my personal assistant.

Mum knew I'd need a car to get to and from work, and certainly didn't want it to be the family Falcon. So she went to Stan Sutherland at the local garage, and bought a 1959 Humber 80. It was a real good one, an absolute minter. Not only was it a ride to and from work, but a ticket to teenage freedom. Provided I'd done what was expected of me on the farm, I could now go where I wanted to. I could watch motorsport, or go down the winding road to Waingaro Hot Springs on a Saturday night – with my cousins Gavin, Karen, and Robbie, Michele Hooten, Carolyn Turner and brother Geoffrey. Gavin was the joke teller of the bunch, a real hard case. He'd crack us up at least once for every one of those 45 kilometres between Pukekawa and Waingaro.

Watching one-day cricket was another interest I developed during those days, and it is still one of my favourite things to do when I'm in the mood to blob out on the couch. Maybe it's the mathematical component to the sport. There are similarities with rallying such as the times when the batsman has to go for it and score runs, and times when they have to be conservative and preserve their wicket. On one of those trips to the Hot Springs we watched New Zealand beat the "Poms" in Australia in the pub next door. The Black Caps batted second, and had to score 314 to win. Lance Cairns hit 44 runs off the final overs to seal the victory while the whole pub went wild. It was one of those moments that you remember all your life to inspire you at times when the task ahead seems impossible.

One evening, when I was 16, I was driving home from work in the Humber on Springhills Road. In the evening sunset I caught a glimpse of a small furry animal running straight across my path. It was a possum. I swerved suddenly to avoid it, lost control on the loose gravel, and rolled the Humber onto its roof. Stunned by the violence of my first car crash, I crawled out of the car through the smashed side window, cutting my arm on the jagged edges of glass. Luckily, it was my only injury, and I walked the rest of the way home to get help. Little did I know then that this crash would be the end of Peter Bourne. From that day on, people called me "Possum".

ANOTHER PERSPECTIVE:

Peggy Bourne, a.k.a. as "Peggy Number 1" by the Bourne family, and "Mummy Possum" by hundreds of rally fans:

I knew something was wrong when I hadn't heard a car, and Peter wandered in. He was as white as sheet, and oozing blood from the cut on his arm where he'd crawled out of the car. We could see he wasn't hurt too badly, and rang Stan Sutherland to

come and look at the car. When he arrived at the scene he declared it a write-off. When Peter told him what had happened, Stan tried hard not to laugh. Most people in New Zealand view possums as an introduced pest, and run them over at any opportunity. Unfortunately for Peter, Stan's son Paul worked in the parts department at Howe and Weston, and quickly spread the news. When Peter showed up for work the next day, everyone started calling him "possum-dodger", and "possum-lover". At the end of the day, the workshop foreman declared that from then on Peter's official work-name was Possum.

Peter took it on the chin at the time, but later, when he started rallying, he told me he couldn't have a better name for attracting the interest of the media.

But to me, he'll always be Peter, and I'm the only one who still calls him by his real name.

Years later, we had a barbecue in Pukekohe for the visiting Subaru 555 team, and Ari Vatanen and Colin McRae were there. I handed Peter a plate of meat in front of Ari, and said:

"Peter, can you take this out to the barbecue?"

Ari said "Peter, who's Peter? Ahh, so that's his real name."

POSSUM IS BORN

My thumb got plenty of exercise after I wrecked the Humber. I'd hitchhike to and from Pokeno for the next six months so I could hook up with my work-mate Gareth, and ride the rest of the way to and from Pukekohe with him. Eventually I saved enough of my wages to buy an old 1957 EIP Vauxhall. It was damaged when I bought it, but a few repairs soon got it back on the road. It was parked outside Howe and Weston's when one of the tractor salesmen ran over it. The tractor mounted the Vauxhall like it was trying to mate with it. I took it to Sutherland's garage in Mercer, where Stan and the guys beat out the damaged panels, and painted it. Looking back, it's a bit of a coincidence that I chose a colour very similar to the bright blue of a factory-supported Subaru rally car.

Despite the colour, the EIP soon showed its limitations. Two of the other apprentices at Howe and Weston, Warren Hull and Steven Fry, were members of the Pukekohe Car Club, and I started attending club meetings with them. I joined as a social member at first, but soon felt the call of competition. I sold the EIP, and bought a 998 cc Mini from Warren. It had twin carbs and a hot cam, and was a great little car for gymkhanas. I even took it to the Meremere dragstrip for a spot of drag-racing.

There wasn't much opportunity for an apprentice to earn the funds to go racing, but that was where my interest lay. Often we'd wag night school to attend a club event, or simply go driving on the back roads because it was more fun. At the club, I'd help out wherever I could, as a start marshall for a rally, or assisting elsewhere. It was a really strong club under the leadership of presidents the calibre of Dave Pilkington and Stu Holmes, with 150 active members and plenty of organised events. It was all good grass-roots fun, even from the sidelines – which was where my apprentice wages kept me.

I soon felt frustrated at Howe and Weston. Not only did they find out about some of the apprentices skylarking instead of attending night school, but also we seemed to be constantly blamed for anything that went wrong. I damaged three customer cars during test-drives during my time there in silly little incidents that weren't entirely my fault. One day a customer bought in his HQ Holden for a warrant-of-fitness test. So I checked the inside of the car, as you do, and took it out on the road and gave it a brake test. Little did I know there were 100 dozen eggs in the boot. I got back to the garage with a gooey mess oozing out of the boot. Every single egg was broken, and the boss tore strips off me. But how was I supposed to know they were there when the customer hadn't told me? I decided to leave H&W as soon as my apprenticeship was finished.

As soon as my time was up, I went to the dairy company and became a tanker driver. Frank Alexander was a great boss who understood my need for time off in the weekends. The money was a quantum leap above that paid to an apprentice mechanic, and I enjoyed driving for a living. Life was good at the dairy company, and the extra funds gave me more confidence as a person. I got over my shyness, and found a girlfriend – Denise Lemon - but it lasted no more than a couple of weeks. Maybe the way I drove scared her off.

I could start contemplating more powerful cars than the Mini. I traded it for a Hillman Hunter, and put a downdraft Weber carburettor on it.

Rallying was having a real impact on the New Zealand car club scene when I joined, reaching new heights of interest with the television coverage of events like the Heatway Rally of New Zealand. I remember watching the 1973 Heatway and thinking that it looked like a lot of fun. So I started getting involved as part of a support crew, first for Rex Dixon and the Anglia van he rallied with co-driver Ken Fricker. Meanwhile, Denise Lemon was now going out with Max Irwin, who also rallied an Anglia.

I knew Max a little as we both had gone to Pukekohe High, but when we each found out the other was mad about cars, the friendship was galvanised. Denise and Max introduced me to Robyn Edwards who became my girlfriend. We'd go out to the Irwin's place near the Waikato River and stay the weekend, the girls chatting away while Max and I worked on our cars in the shed. Max's parents, Yvonne and Eddie Irwin, started treating me like a second son.

Max asked me if I'd like to be his co-driver in a Pukekohe car club rally. Now, I'm someone who much prefers driving to being driven. Back then, I was always happy not to drink at a social event, and stay sober to drive the gang home, albeit with a few skids on the way. But I was so keen to get into rallying, and this was my earliest opportunity. Max was an absolute natural when it came being a talented wheelman, whereas I wasn't displaying any raw driving ability at that stage. My first effort at chucking the Hillman sideways was a near-disaster. I over-corrected one way, then the next, and sent the thing into a tank-slapper. It took a few more club hillclimbs in the Hunter to get my eye in. I'd forge Dad's signature on the entry form because I was under the age of consent.

Max and I finished sixth in the rally, which included a special stage over Springhills Road. Although there were no pace notes, that was one stage where my local knowledge helped. The road

I grew up on definitely influenced the sporting direction I was taking. I discovered early that skidding a car on gravel was fun, and joining the car club gave me the opportunity to do it without being such a menace to the public. When Max asked me if I'd like to race the Anglia in a car club hillclimb up Chamberlain Road, there was no hesitation in accepting.

On the day, Mum turned up to watch, but said she had her eyes closed the whole time when the Anglia came by.

By now the desire to compete was overwhelming. I sold the Hillman, and bought a Holden Torana XU1 as my road car. This down-under derivative of the humble Vauxhall Viva was every Australasian teenager's dream machine at the time. Powered by a 3.0 litre straight six stoked by three Zenith sidedraft carbs, the XU1 was a 1030 kgs compact sedan with 160 brake horsepower under the bonnet. The XU1 had a limited slip rear diff, and went like stink.

It was the car that taught me to drive. I wasn't much into drinking and socialising on the weekends. Instead Michael Eggleton and I would take the Torana out on the gravel roads all around Pukekohe on Friday and Saturday nights, and try to get the hang of the thing. There are lots of blind corners on those roads, and doing it at night gave us the opportunity to see the lights of any oncoming traffic. That way we avoided causing any grief. We went anywhere there was a gravel road – out to

Karaka, to the heads of the Manukau harbour, or over the Waikato River. I never raced it, but the rear tyres would never last more than 6000 kilometres.

The XU1 was too good to go rallying or hillclimbing with, so I bought a Cortina V8 from Dave Dixon. It had a 3.5 litre Oldsmobile V8 under the bonnet, but the increased power and torque was hard on the driveline. I found this out the hard way. I kept the Cortina at Ken Fricker's garage in Karaka, and he had a Maori guy, Jack Carney, working for him. Jack was a big bloke; he played prop for the Ardmore rugby team and weighed around 19 stone. We took the Cortina for a run to check it out for a coming hillclimb, Jack sitting on an apple box instead of in a proper seat. I used to take people for rides on that apple box at the time, and my sister Deb said it was the thrill of a lifetime. I was young, thought I was bulletproof, and didn't think of the consequences until that one day in Bombay, south of Auckland.

We were drifting the Cortina around a corner when the rear axle broke. The sudden locking of the rear wheels tripped the car over, and Jack, with no seat belt to secure him, got chucked out the back window. He was hurt, but not too badly. It was an absolute miracle that he was still alive and didn't break a bone. It was a loud wake-up call for me, and taught me a big lesson about racing on public roads. The police gave me a serious talking to, but didn't lay any charges. They said the marks on the road showed how hard I was going when the axle broke, and that there was a case for me to have my road licence disqualified for dangerous driving. By then, they were preaching to the converted. The thought that I came so close to killing Jack made me grow up in a hurry, and a maturer driver emerged from that accident. When the car club suspended my competition licence for a couple of months, I thought it was the right thing to do.

The break from competition gave me the opportunity to sort out the Cortina. We got another body shell to tidy it up, and started beefing up the drive-train so it could handle a full rally rather than just the short burst of a hillclimb. Max had dropped a similar V8 into an Escort, and came up with the idea that we should melt aluminium and put it in the Wolseley diffs we were using to lock them. This gave us more reliability. For the suspension I installed the front uprights, springs and Bilstein shocks from a World Cup Escort, and had to fabricate my own bottom arms because of the wider wheel tracks of the Cortina. I also put in the World Cup Escort's pedal box and quicker steering rack as well. With the V8 sucking fuel through a four-barrel Holley carb, and driving a Mark IV Zodiac gearbox, it was a pretty smart little car. It weighed 1005 kilos and developed 260 horsepower. The finishing touches were some Bridgestone Timesaver tyres.

Allan Woolf, a great saloon car racer, and a staunch supporter of rallying and hillclimbing in New Zealand, couldn't believe the competitiveness of the Pukekohe boys when he showed up at one of our hillclimbs. There was Neil Allport, Max Irwin, Ken Fricker, Reg Cook, Neil Laurent, Tony Teesdale and Michael Eggelton and I going at it hammer and tongs. There was such depth to the driving talent at the club, and several of these guys could have gone onto international rally careers. Neil Allport and Reg did make a big impact at a national level, but most had the talent to go further in the sport.

Take Max, for example; he was probably the pick of them all, and could have gone to the top had the family farm not distracted him. Drop him in anything and he'd drive it to its full potential, and do it safely. But to him it was just a sport, something to do after work, whereas for me it was rapidly becoming something I wanted to do for a living. When "Woolfie", the sponsor of the hillclimb, got up to give his speech at the prize-giving afterward, he said every competitor was driving so hard on the day that it must be a club rule that the loser had to shout the rest at the bar!

If people told me "You're mad", I took it as a compliment. It showed that I was driving right on the edge, and it made me feel like I had an edge by being the maddest joker in the pack. The guy I remember saying it most often was Laurie Powell, one of the club officials. At one hillclimb Laurie was casually sitting on a hay-bale on the exit to the last bend. When I came by, full-opposite-lock, inside front wheel a foot in the air, with the V8 spitting gravel, he tossed himself backwards over the bale to get out of the way. When I finished the run, he wasted no time in coming over to remind me what he thought of my mental health. My response – an ear-to-ear grin – must have confirmed his suspicions.

Hillclimbing taught me to go hard right from the start – to find the racing line first time out, and keep the car on the limit right from start to finish. Rallying isn't so good at teaching you how to find more speed, because you're on your own, and it's personal motivation that drives your speed. Whereas hillclimbs are short, and you're talking to your competition between runs, geeing each other along and bluffing that you've got more speed to come with the next run. It teaches you skills on where to find more speed, because you go over the same stretch of road several times. You take those skills to a rally and you come out and do the stage right first time. The downside is that hillclimbing teaches you to go hard or go home. For some time I couldn't get into a car without driving the arse off it.

Going rallying was definitely the best chance I had for a professional motorsport career. I looked to people like Allan Woolf's son John, Rod Millen, and Paul Adams for inspiration. By 1979, Rod was starting to make a name for himself in the US, and John and Paul had one of the most professional rally teams in New Zealand with sponsorship from Nylex Industries for their Mazda RX-3 and Escort RS1800. When the factory teams came down to New Zealand for the international rally, these guys made sure they kept them on their toes. To follow in their footsteps meant taking the plunge and taking on the extra expense that rallying represented. There were tyres, fuel, travel and accommodation to consider, while Mum helped out by loading up chilly bins with Tupperware containers full of food. She'd bake for days before a rally. With a fresh set of Timesavers underneath us, co-driver Ken Fricker and I fronted up in the Cortina V8 for my first rally as a driver: the 1979 Woodhill Forest event organised by the Northern Sports Car Club.

I was so nervous at the start that my stomach started doing flips. This was something that would take years to get out of my system – start-line nerves that made me feel physically sick. We were seeded 61st in the field, but made a good start, and immediately began passing cars. As we moved up the field, I began to relax. Then came the moment that defined my life. I pitched the Cortina hard through a bend, and in a long line between the pine trees, an ultra-fast straight opened up in front of us. As we accelerated down it, the V8 singing at high revs, accompanied by the scattergun pinging of the stones on the underside of the car, I remember thinking, "Hey, I've finally found it." Finally I'd found what I wanted to do with my life. From that moment on rallying was the most fun, most cool thing I could ever do, and a quiet determination came over me to do it to the best of my ability.

With the V8 pushing the ancient Cortina up to high speeds on Woodhill's long straights, Frick and I cut a swathe through the field. We finished third after a sensational run, behind Tony Teesdale and Morrie Chandler.

The next rally in the Cortina V8 wasn't so successful, although we still showed our potential. At a Hamilton Car Club rally in Pureora Forest, the distributor broke on the engine, dropping us down to 33rd place, although we set times in the fastest top five every other stage. If you took that one stage out where the distributor broke, we would have finished second.

Then we fluked a win at the MG Car Club rally in Riverhead Forest. It showed just how good the Cortina V8 was. It was fast and light, and right on the pace of the Mazda RX-3s and RS1800 Escorts that were the rally cars of choice at the time. I've still got the Cortina in my shed at home, but it retired from rallying on a winning note in 1979. It was time to get serious about the National Rally Championship, and for that I needed a car that was eligible rather than a home-built hybrid.

Hanging out at Woolfie's gave me good insight into the relative merits of the Escort versus the Mazda as the Nylex team ran both. The Ford was the more complete car, with better brakes and suspension, but it required more maintenance and cost more to run. The Mazda, with a 13B rotary engine tuned by either Bill Shiells or John Woolf, had the potential for more speed, and the rotary engine didn't need the constant attention of the highly-strung Ford. I sold the XU1, and used the money to buy an ex-Rod Millen four-door RX-3 from Owen Evans. The Shiells-tuned engine could rev out to 9,000 rpm, and propel the RX-3 to a top speed of 240 km/h, 16 km/h more than the fastest Escorts. It was just a pity the pathetic little brakes couldn't haul it up as fast as the Ford. And I'd find out early that the air filter needed constant attention.

At a rally sprint on a grass-track I seized the engine. I was driving hard in the dust, and finding the handling of the RX-3 hard work after the Cortina, when it suddenly stopped. With John's help we re-built the motor in time for the 1980 Woodhill Forest Rally, and he gave me a few tips on preserving the rotary – things he'd learned while establishing a fine finishing record in the international rally. As long as I didn't rev the ring off the thing, kept the fuel mixture slightly rich to preserve the seals, and the air filter pristine, the rotary would do a whole rally season just with the occasional oil change.

Frick and I had a short Woodhill Rally. We were second fastest on the first stage after Jim Donald, but I missed the finish line, and suddenly found people everywhere. So I hit the brakes hard, and we speared off the road into a tree. The RX-3 wasn't a pretty sight afterward.

John, in his final rally in New Zealand, won, driving Clive Pegden's Mazda with Clive in the co-driver's seat. It was much-needed pocket money for his coming US rally championship campaign with regular co-driver Grant Whittaker. They'd already shipped their black RX-3 stateside, and would go on to take the US scene by storm. With Millen already an established star there, John and Rod were dubbed "the Kiwi Mafia" for the way they took control of the US rally season. John and Grant had intended to compete there until their money ran out, but they kept winning enough rallies to attract support first from Mazda North America, and then Peugeot.

Their rally in the ex-works Peugeot 504 V6 Coupe on May 29, 1982 in Paris, Texas, would be their last event. First on the road, they drove head-on into a large 4wd support vehicle that had strayed onto the stage. It was news so tragic that you always remember where you were when you first heard it. I had just got home from a rally when my first wife Lynne told me what had happened. American journalist Tim Cline spoke for all who knew John and Grant when he wrote: "They were not great celebrities. Not great sports heroes. Their names were not household words. But to those of us who knew and loved them, these two warm and gentle men were the very best the sport had to offer. Of all the people I have known in this sport, they loved it the most."

John and Grant were an inspiration in the way they devoted all their resources to their rallying. Ken and I adopted the same approach to the 1980 season, but it was always touch-and-go whether we made the startline. Just the up-front costs of competing in an event came to $1000, and we'd consume about $1200 worth of tyres in the long-distance events that were the fashion in those days. We had a bit of sponsorship from Statesman Shirts and Giltrap Mazda, but it was a few hundred bucks here and a few hundred bucks there. So any dreams that we might have a chance of winning the championship were always tempered by the reality that we couldn't afford to do the South Island rounds.

Still, we showed our potential. At the Cibie Lights Rally, we posted an equal-fastest time with Jim Donald on the opening stage, and served notice that our 1979 success in the Cortina V8 hadn't been due just to the car. We held second place through the early stages of the rally, but got lost in the Maramarua Forest. It was our first night rally, and we realised that we were out of our depth. By the time we backed up and found the course again, seventh place was all we could race for. But our early efforts in the rally got us noticed by the media, and that's critical to getting anywhere in this sport.

A month later, I finished second to Brian Watkin in the Pukekohe Club Rally after a real ding-dong battle with Max that saw us both go off the road in the final stage. We'd pulled a huge gap on the rest of the field, but Ken and I got back on the road to finish runner-up, while Max retired for an early shower.

At the Hella Lights Rally, fourth round of the national championship, Ken and I set the fastest time on three stages, and posted several other times in the top five, before dropping out mid-way. There was an intense level of talent around at the time. In the top tier were guys like Jim Donald, Mike Marshall, Tony Teesdale, and Paul Adams – well organised drivers who had attracted a high level of support because of their experience and sure-bet results. Below them were a bunch of wild-eyed up-and-comers capable of producing an upset win if their more limited funds allowed it – bloody fast drivers like Blair Robson, Howard Collier and Mark Parsons. Ken and I were competitive on the roads we already knew, but when we left the top half of the North Island, we just got flogged. When we finished in the top 10 at the Hawke's Bay round of the championship, I knew winning it was going to be harder than I first thought. Going south of the Waikato was like a trip to Mars for me.

For the 1981 season, we decided an RX-3 Coupe would offer better handling, so we sold the ex-Millen four door, and built up a car out of a wrecked two-door RX-3. If I'd known then what I know now, I'd have made a better job of it, but the car was still a winner in its first rally. We finished building the car at 9.30

on the night before the first Woodhill Forest round of the Top Half Rally Championship, jumped in it the next day, and won every stage. We finished a minute ahead of runner-up Mike Limbrick, followed by Reece Jones, Neill Allport, Mark Parsons, and Morrie Chandler.

We weren't planning to do the international rally that year, but with the Woodhill win front sports page news in the *New Zealand Herald*, it was a good time to canvas the Pukekohe and Papakura business communities for their support. In all, 66 names were painted in yellow on the bonnet of the black RX-3, after my sister Kristine, Ken and I knocked on doors and asked for support. Mum was surprised to see her name there, but, hey, she gave me plenty of help, reaching into her pocket any time I needed a part. The whip-round gave us $5000 – enough to lodge an entry on the 1981 Motogard Rally of New Zealand under the "Spirit of South Auckland" banner. In the rally we held fourth position until the third day, when we crashed out of third place in the Pureora Forest. For the hard-working crew of Merv Perry, Kevin Hamilton, Rodney Atchinson, Michael Eggelton, and Colin Lever, it was a poor return for their efforts.

We consoled ourselves by winning the Pukekohe Club Rally, the final round of the Top Half Championship, after fending off another strong challenge from Max in the Escort V8. Tony Teesdale gathered enough points to win the championship in his BDA Escort, with Reece Jones runner-up in his Mazda RX-3.

The 1982 season didn't get off to a great start, but it could have been worse.

A puncture slowed our defence of the Woodhill win, and although we charged through the final stages, we still finished four seconds short of winner Peter Farrell. Things took a turn for the better in the Pukekohe round of the Top Half series, when Ken and I won the rally by half a minute from Neil Allport, although Neil put up a strong fight at first.

We did just one round of the national championship – the Auckland-based Hella Lights Rally – where we finished third after stopping to assist Tony Teesdale and co-driver Greg Horne who had had a horrible crash in their Escort. Being second on the scene, there was no obligation to stop, but it was immediately obvious that this was a serious accident. Greg was hurt badly, and we took him out of the stage to a waiting ambulance. The officials assessed my potential time for that stage, and awarded me third place at the rally's end. They also gave me a sportsmanship award, with a welcome $200 cheque from Dunlop tyres. A month later a $2000 cheque arrived from Dunlop when I was named "Driver of the Year." The third place, combined with the rescue effort, was evidently enough to win the title.

My last drive in the RX-3 took place in May 1983, when I completed a hat-trick of victories in the Pukekohe Rally with Radio New Zealand's Ian Woodley in the co-driver's seat. However, with the growing dominance of the Audi Quattro in the World Rally Championship, the writing was on the wall for rear-wheel-drive cars. When I wandered past Don Thomson's Subaru showroom in Pukekohe, and spied the new 4wd RX Turbo Coupe, I immediately saw an affordable substitute for the mighty Quattro. So I went inside and asked Don whether he'd be interested in supporting me in a RX Turbo campaign. He immediately rang Subaru New Zealand boss Geoff Cousins to see what he thought of his dealership sponsoring a local Pukekohe driver.

"Yeah, we're thinking of getting into rallying," said Geoff, "but there's only enough money for one car, and we're only interested in getting involved with that Possum Bourne guy."

"Well, he's sitting on the other side of my desk," Don replied.

OTHER PERSPECTIVES:

Max Irwin – Escort V8 pilot:

When Possum started turning up at our place, I'd worry about my tools.

He'd work on his car outside on the grass, and if it was time to go to work, he'd just leave everything lying out there. But I never could get mad at him. It wouldn't have worked anyway. He was just so happy-go-lucky, and nothing seemed to faze him.

He was absolutely mad about rallying and cars. He said to me "One day they'll pay me to drive."

I said "Yeah, right. Not even Rod Millen (who was a draughtsman at the time) gets paid to drive."

He's certainly proved me wrong since.

His sheer enthusiasm for the sport encouraged us all, but it cost him dearly when it came to girlfriends. One Saturday night, Possum was supposed to take Robyn to a wedding dance, and she'd gone out and bought an expensive new dress for the occasion. Possum turned up at our house instead, and we had a few beers and started talking about cars. At 11 p.m. he suddenly realised the time, slapped his forehead, and said: "Oh shit, I was supposed to pick Robyn up at eight."

He didn't keep her long.

Possum was frightening as a driver in those early years, as his courage far outweighed his skill. If someone did a nice handbrake slide, he'd have to do it at twice the speed, and usually stuffed it up. When he went hillclimbing, he'd leave bits of the car behind all the way up the run. When you saw a car heading for the finish line with bits of gorse stuck in the each corner of a crumpled rear bumper, you knew immediately who was driving it. Before a hill climb, my mother used to give him a lecture:

"Now you will drive sensibly this time, won't you Possum? You won't bring back a wrecked car this time will you? You know you can't afford the repairs..."

The only time I saw Possum take fright was when Mum caught him driving her beloved ride-on mower around the milking shed on two wheels. We thought she was out, and took it down there to do time trials around the pipework. She snuck up on us just as it was his go, and tore him to shreds. He took a while to get over that one.

On the first rally where he co-drove in the Anglia, Possum was so enthused it was like he was driving. He kept yelling: "Keep it flat, the corner straightens up." We nearly cabbaged the car a couple of times when it didn't. When we finished, we were both chuffed, and he said, "That's it, I'm going rallying."

I said, "You're crazy, can't you see how much it's costing me."

It was always very competitive between us, and it really came to a head at the Pukekohe Rally in 1980. We both went mad, and nearly crashed every stage. By the last stage we had a huge lead on the rest of the field and Possum had about two seconds on me. However, I thought I knew the last stage better than him, so I was confident of winning. Possum went first in the RX-3, and I followed a minute later in the Escort V8. There was this long straight, and the V8 hit the 7500 rpm rev limiter in top gear, which I knew meant we were going 230 km/h. I backed off for the coming corner, and thought I heard my co-driver, Mike Taylor, say: "Too soon."

So I got straight back on the gas again, because I just had to beat him. We hit the corner with way too much speed and went straight into the ditch. Mike was keen to get going again, and some spectators came running over to help us. But I'd had enough.

"I didn't put in all this effort to finish second," I yelled.

Little did I know Possum was over in a ditch, a further 150 metres up the road. He'll never let me live it down that I chucked in the towel.

Peggy Bourne, Possum's Mum:

All these car club guys would turn up sometimes when Possum was working on his car at our house. He'd introduce them just by their nicknames saying: "this is 'Strut' and this is 'Plank'" and so on. They were the nicest blokes, and Ray and I really enjoyed having them around. One day a woman I knew well rang up to ask if her son Kevin was there. I said: "Kevin, who's Kevin?" It was then that the penny dropped that I'd been feeding Mrs Hamilton's son "Hammy" for some time.

The only one who ever annoyed Ray was "Plank", who one night after he'd had a few too many beers decided it was a good idea to do some wheelies in his car around the hay paddock. Ray was livid the next morning. All the other times we enjoyed the social spirit of the guys, and the way they'd all pitch in to help each other out.

When I first watched Possum race, I kept my eyes closed. However the next time I found myself screaming "Boot it Peter!" when he came past.

When he started winning, Ray was ever so proud of his son. When he broke down or crashed, probably no one felt the disappointment more than his Dad.

Kristine Game, Possum's sister and personal assistant:
Most big brothers look after their little sisters, but it was a case of role reversal with Peter and me. I'd later become his personal assistant, and the chief organiser of his calendar, but in the early days roles I willingly accepted included looking after Ken's garage in Karaka when they went away rallying, and loaning Peter my car when he needed to take a girl out.

He couldn't afford his own car as well as a rally car, so I'd fill my Mark II Cortina up with gas, and nine times out of 10, it'd come back to me empty. One time it came back with a damaged radiator. He'd give me the keys to a ratty old Transit van in exchange, and it'd break down and leave me stranded at worst possible moments.

I was happy to lend him the Cortina because I was as passionate about his rallying as he was, and it was a way I could give him some support. Besides, it kept me up with the "goss" on his love life. The Bournes can be a sarcastic bunch at times, but we'll always be there for one another in times of need. We can also be a bit intimidating. Such as when we went to watch him in the Woodhill Rally and met his new girlfriend Lynne Stephens for the first time.

He had told her, "Don't worry, if they don't like you, they'll soon tell you." This made her twice as nervous about meeting us.

DRIVING WITH THE STARS

Don's call to Geoff took place late on a Friday evening. The following Monday morning I was round at Motor Holdings Limited's head office in Auckland as early as I could to strike before Geoff changed his mind. Over the weekend, I'd put together a budget to do a season for Subaru. Geoff accepted the proposal, installed Laurie Inskeep as the team manager (i.e. keeper of the company credit card for our expenses), and said it was a one-off deal that would be reviewed at the end of the year.

If Geoff Cousins hadn't given me a chance to drive the Subaru, it would have been the end of my dream to be a professional rally driver. It was to be a one-off drive that would last 20 years, and still counting. Over the next two decades, every car I'd rally would bear the star-crusted badge of the Subaru brand. It'd be hard to find any other professional driver in motorsport who stayed loyal to the one-car company for that long.

The Subaru New Zealand deal was a dream come true, for it happened at the perfect time for me. At 27, I was ready to put down some roots, and Lynne seemed the ideal partner. Although she supported my rallying, she may have thought it was

something I'd "grow out of" eventually. She'd seen me burn plenty of money in two seasons with the Mazdas. Rallying is a tough mistress for wives and partners to compete with, and it's driven plenty of marriages to the divorce courts, mainly because of the demands it places on family finances. Getting the Subaru drive meant we could now think about buying a house together, and, eventually, the RX-3 would be sold to place a deposit on a house in the country between Pukekohe and Bombay.

When I met Lynne she was a receptionist at D&W Ford, the Pukekohe dealership. Soon I was working there as well, as a mechanic in the workshop. Although Frank Alexander tried hard at the dairy company to ensure I had time off for rallying, the six-day shifts there were too demanding. Moving to D&W Ford gave me definite weekends, and after work we'd work on the rallycar, often into the small hours of the morning. This didn't go down well with the workshop foreman. Half his staff would turn up the next day looking like they'd had just a couple of hours sleep. So, soon I was back truck-driving again – for Jim and John Evans. They were always willing to give me time off when I needed it.

58

Noel Robinson, who used to go to night school with me as an apprentice, and joined the Pukekohe Car Club at the same time, also worked for J&J Evans at times when they needed a hand. He leased Ken Fricker's garage in Karaka, and did contract work for Don Thomson's Subaru dealership. Noel, Snow Mooney, Merv Perry, Kevin and John Hamilton, and Neil Laurent formed the backbone of the team. Our first job was to sort the car for the coming Sanyo International Rally of New Zealand. We selected a white RX Leone Coupe, and pulled it apart to modify it for rallying. In went a full roll cage, while the stock 85 horsepower 1.8 litre engine was sent to Reg Cook for the modifications permitted under Group A class rules. With just 85 brake horses driving a heavy car equipped with power-sapping 4wd, the engine needed all the help we could find for it. However, when it came back from Reg, the motor was a huge disappointment. The team's support utes were faster than the rallycar!

Reg, inspired by the Mini Cooper S, had ground up a similar-looking camshaft for the Subaru. It didn't work, and when we handed the motor over to Tony "Swampy" Marsh, he put the stock camshaft back in, and it went a lot better. However, it still didn't have much guts. Compared to the RX-3, it could have been a Morrie Minor. I found I had to bank away any momentum like it was precious gold if we were to set competitive stage times. Gone was the spectacular tail-hanging-out-wide style associated with the name "Possum Bourne", replaced by a smoother, less dramatic performance encouraged by the extra grip of four-wheel-drive. I couldn't believe how much more grip the Subaru had when cornering and braking, and it was hard to adjust my driving style to it at first.

So Geoff was quite nervous when the Sanyo Rally started. He wondered whether this effort to break Subaru out of the "farmer's car" mould would backfire on the brand. Certainly the comments of rally fans didn't help his confidence. They saw my move to Subaru as a backward step at first, and weren't shy about voicing their opinion that I could have gone faster in the Mazda.

However, Ken and I were quite happy with the move. We knew that if we didn't secure manufacturer or distributor support for our efforts, then we could only aim at winning club rallies. We saw Group A – a more production-car based formula – as the future of rallying, and in Subaru we had found a supporter for our efforts, and a manufacturer at the leading edge of four-wheel-drive technology. Until Subaru started using 4wd in road cars, there was a perception in New Zealand that it was technology that only had some worth when driving off-road. Rally success was a great illustration of its worth in local road conditions, and what Audi would prove with the Quattro by dominating the 1983 international season, we aimed to do locally with Subaru. It didn't matter to us that the car was slow at first. We knew a Japanese manufacturer like Subaru would soon develop more powerful engines if it recognised rallying as an excellent marketing tool.

The Leone RX Coupe had already proved to be a reliable rallycar in the East African Safari by finishing fifth and eleventh overall, and first and third in Group A. It underlined that reputation in the Sanyo Rally of New Zealand. It was a long rally in those days – with more than 1100 kilometres of special stages – and although the field was a strong one, Ken and I soon started moving up the order. I remember passing the stricken factory Audi Quattro of Michele Mouton somewhere in the Bay of Plenty hinterland. Walter Rohrl won in his Lancia Rallye after Stig Blomqvist was excluded in the rapid Renault 5 Turbo. We finished fourteenth overall, and first in Group A. Geoff was overjoyed to have something to boast about. Next day, full-page Subaru ads in New Zealand newspapers carried the statement that "the technology that wins rallies can be driven away from the showroom". Subaru sales rose by 25 percent in New Zealand that year, convincing Geoff that the time-honoured "race on Sunday, sell on Monday" method of brand-building was working.

Our effort in New Zealand helped Subaru secure eighth place in the manufacturer's section of the World Rally Championship, opening up doors to us in Japan. We had a virtually trouble-free run over the gruelling event, replacing just the tyres, brake pads, rear shocks, and a suspension strut. The only real drama happened to Snow. He rolled the support ute in the darkness of the Kaingaroa Forest, near Rotorua, and knocked himself out. It took a while to find him, and get him to an ambulance, and a rally fan with a Holden ute was quickly recruited to take his place in the team. Snow checked himself out of the hospital the next day, and started walking towards Pukekohe while still wearing his hospital gown! Fortunately his parents drove down and picked him up before someone rang the police to say a lunatic had escaped from the asylum.

The Subaru used even fewer parts in the national Cibie Lights Rally, flying through the event without a change of anything but tyres. Ken and I were seeded 17th, but soon started moving up the field over the eleven stages. We finished fourth overall, and third in class C, behind the Nissans of Reg Cook and Tony Teesdale. The 240RS and Sylvia driven by Reg and Tony had twice the horsepower of the RX, but not the traction advantage of all-wheel-drive. It was a result that really got other teams taking the Subaru seriously, along with our class B win in the second round of the North Island Rally Championship – where we finished eighth overall.

In the final round of the national championship – the Hella Lights Rally – the Subaru had its first major breakdown when the gearbox packed a sad. The crew quickly changed the gearbox in record time at the side of the road, but the replacement wasn't the close-ratio transmission we were used to. Handicapped by the larger gaps between gears, we finished 11th overall in the final rally of the '83 season, and sixth in Group A. We consoled ourselves with third place in the final rallysprint of the year – an event unlikely to suit a lowly Group A car – finishing just half a second behind runner-up Neil Allport in an Escort RS1800.

Our 1983 performance as a team – both on the road, and in the service areas where we performed tasks like the Hella Lights gearbox swap in record time – didn't go unnoticed at Subaru's headquarters in Shinjuku, Tokyo. For the 1984 international, a factory-developed RX Coupe was shipped out to us, arriving on the same boat as a special Toyota Corolla for Group A rival Paul Adams. The factory Subaru engine, stoked by a down-draft Weber carburettor for each arm of the boxer four, developed nearly twice the power of a stock Leone RX Coupe engine at 160 bhp. Now we were cooking with gas!

The other big change took place in the co-driver's seat. We were finally allowed to use pace notes for the first time, and Ken had too many business commitments to go driving over stages every weekend to sort out the notes. So Michael Eggleton took his place. We'd drive thousands of kilometres every weekend, and try to write a set of notes that were worthwhile. I thought it was a huge waste of time at first, especially as Michael was prone to car-sickness. There were times when eating Minties made a difference for him, and others when they made no difference at all, and we needed to stop frequently so he could empty his upset stomach. During rallies, Michael would undo his belts, and open the door to have a heave with the car going flat chat. He'd yell at me if I slowed down. Sometimes there wasn't the opportunity to do this, so he'd simply vomit in his lap. He soon gave up wearing full-face helmets for the open face models! When we finished a stage, and someone wanted to ask us how we went, they'd always approach the car via the driver's side. It was a pity about Michael's constitution, because he was an excellent co-driver in all other respects.

The pace notes began to make sense once Michael and I developed our own system for calling the corners. We used the amount I had to turn the wheel to determine the sharpness of the bend, and assigned a number to it. A "4" meant I had to turn the wheel 90 degrees, a "5" was half that at 45 degrees, a 6 half that again, and so on. So a "3" required 180 degrees of wheel movement, a "2" a full turn.

However, I was still a bit sceptical about the notes when the Sanyo Rally of New Zealand kicked off on the first gravel stages in Woodhill Forest. After Michael called this tricky corner correctly two kilometres into the first stage, he turned to me and said: "These notes are fantastic".

And they really were. They filled me with so much confidence about where we were going, and how hard I should chuck the car into the bends. By the end of the first stage we'd beaten the current New Zealand rally champion Tony Teesdale in the same car by half a minute. We absolutely flogged Paul Adams in the factory-prepared Corolla as well as any other contender for the Group A prize. These guys were also using pace notes, but they hadn't developed a system as good as ours. As we flew through the 1000 kilometre rally to eighth place overall, and first in Group A, I wondered why rally chief official Morrie Chandler had held the sport back so long by not allowing the use of pace notes in New Zealand.

It was a huge result, especially as there were people from the Subaru head office in Japan there to witness it. We finished the rally 16 minutes ahead of Tony Teesdale who had another factory prepared RX. When Paul Adams dropped out, and Bruce Powell finished 19th overall in a Group A Leone, it gave Subaru a clean sweep of the class. Up front, in Group B, Lancia driver Markku Alen stopped Audi dominating the podium by finishing five minutes behind winner Stig Blomqvist, and three minutes ahead of Hannu Mikkola. Reg Cook was first New Zealander home in sixth place overall.

The Group A win scored me the Dunlop Driver of the Event award, worth $500. At the season's end, Dunlop awarded me another $2000 cheque as rally driver of the year, after Michael and I won the Group A class in four of the six national rallies we entered. With the help of sponsorship from the Shipping Corporation of New Zealand we competed for the first time in a South Island rally at the South Canterbury Car Club round in Timaru. It was 617 kilometres long and 364 of them were rugged special stages, but we had a pretty clean run to sixth overall, and first Group A car home. The only incident was hitting a large wallaby on the ninth stage. It was big enough to be called a kangaroo! Although I swerved to avoid it, it suddenly changed direction and ran straight into the Subaru, causing some minor damage. At least I didn't miss it and roll the car in doing so. Otherwise you might be calling me "Skippy" Bourne right now.

Crashing out in the final Hella Lights Rally of the championship cost us the 1984 National Group A title. When the points were totalled, our account had a deficit of five compared with that of Bruce McKenzie and his Toyota Corolla. I felt I'd let the sponsors and the team down with that DNF. They'd hired me to be a reliable driver, and it was no way to repay their support. However, the Driver of the Year award soon cheered me up. Especially as the cheque arrived the day before Lynne and I got married. We settled into the house we bought together with the proceeds from the RX-3 sale, and I stopped truck-driving to begin a new job as a sales rep for Lucas.

Selling lights and other electrical parts and accessories was good practice in public relations. I'd earn kudos as Lucas's best-selling sales rep, helped by the doors my name in rallying opened for me. I'd call on a customer, chat about rallying, and they'd give me an order. It was as easy as shooting fish in a barrel. Lucas were happy to be involved in rallying as well, and their lights soon found their way onto the Subaru. Getting time off to go racing wasn't an issue.

I was determined to make amends for the poor performance in the 1984 Hella Lights when the 1985 New Zealand Rally Championship started in Southland. Held in June, in the part of the South Island closest to Antarctica, a southerly-propelled storm made the roads snowy, icy, and slippery. This created perfect conditions for the all-wheel-drive Subaru. It was misty and miserable going into the second stage of the rally – a stage I'll always remember as one of the best I ever drove. We started fourth on the road, but emerged first after passing the Audi Quattro of Malcolm Stewart, the Nissan 240RS of Tony Teesdale, and the Escort RS2000 of Hugh Owen. They were Group B cars with a lot more horsepower than ours, but while they were driving gingerly through the fog, we were charging. At the end of the stage, a reporter came running up and asked how I'd coped with the icy, foggy conditions.

"What fog?" I replied, "I didn't notice any."

Thanks to Michael's accurate notes, the statement was true. He was one of the best co-drivers I drove with – it was just a shame about his motion sickness.

That second stage performance in Southland set up Subaru's first overall win in the New Zealand Rally Championship. We could almost hear the distant cheering in Shinjuku. The only other driver to keep us in sight was Paul Adams in the Group A Toyota, who finished second overall. The Group B guys must have wondered what the world was coming to with two production-based cars beating their purpose-built rally cars.

The win in Southland was the swansong for the normally-aspirated RX Coupe. For the next event was the AWA Clarion Rally of New Zealand, and the newly-set-up Subaru Motorsports Group put on a show of strength for the international. A fleet of five newly-developed RX Turbo Group A Coupes arrived. Two for Tony Teesdale and me, and three for East African Safari exponents Mike Kirkland, Carlo Vittuli, and Frank Tundo. With Aussie driver Ed Milligan also entering in a Leone RX Turbo, there was plenty of competition for Group A honours just within the Subaru camp, let alone the other teams.

The turbocharged engine gave us around 40 more horsepower than the old car, so we were now playing with 200 bhp. The car had a larger "footprint" thanks to wider wheel tracks, giving us the opportunity to dial out understeer. Once we fashioned our own suspension lower arms, we could crank up some negative camber and make the car more responsive to the wheel.

When Michael and I led all the other Group A cars home to finish eighth overall, Mike Kirkland said to me: "You should do more international rallies, why don't you come to Kenya and do the Safari next year?"

The simple answer was money, or rather, the lack of it. But Mike wasn't going to take "No, thanks" for a reply. The next thing I knew, he was pulling strings with the Japanese. They had huge respect for Mike's experience, and always listened to his advice, especially Subaru boss Yoshio Takioka. I'm not sure whether Mike put his hand in his pocket to seal the deal, but next thing there was the offer of a 1986 Safari drive on the table. Subaru would meet all the car expenses, all I had to do was meet all the food, accommodation and travel costs for me and my team.

A rough calculation showed I'd need at least $10,000 to do the Safari. While Lucas would give me time off to attend, it'd still amount to five weeks without pay. When I mentioned the possibility of doing the Safari to Lynne, she wasn't too happy about the prospect. The cracks in our marriage were already starting to show just six months after we tied the knot. Rallying was the big issue, and all the time I spent away from her – working on the car late into the night, or driving some special stage six times over just to make sure the pace notes were right.

Besides, I couldn't contemplate competing offshore while there was a possibility of winning the New Zealand Rally Championship. The win in Southland put us in contention for winning the main title, let alone the Group A crown. We took the RX Turbo to third place overall in the Lucas Lights Rally in Auckland, but had the result thrown out when the officials found the factory-supplied exhaust pipe broke Group A rules.

At the next round in Hawke's Bay, wet slippery conditions came to our aid again, and we finished second overall to Malcolm Stewart's Group B Audi Quattro. We were first Group A car home. In the penultimate round in Taupo, you could have chucked a blanket over the first three cars. Neil Allport won by just 28 seconds from Reg Cook, with Michael and I finishing a further five seconds behind. If we pulled off a fifth place overall finish in the final rally of the year, or better, I'd win the championship, such was the strength of our points lead.

In the final result, we snatched defeat from the jaws of victory. At the Hella Lights Rally in the Coromandel, we led the rally until stage four, where the Subaru's engine started overheating. We'd been under strict instructions from the factory not to touch it, so we couldn't carry out any preventative maintenance through the season. When the temperature gauge started to soar, our hearts sank. We were so close to winning the title, so close to making history for Subaru. We got so desperate to get to the finish, we started using one of the team's utes to push the car through the transport sections, but it was to no avail. The motor coughed its last breath, and we pulled out of the rally.

So we ended the 1985 season third overall, and first in Group A. Subaru rued their decision on the engine many times over. They'd chuck far more resources our way the following year now that we showed them just how close we could come to winning a national rally championship.

Out of the 1985 defeat, the Subaru Motorsports Group was formed. For 1986 there would be a whole new deal, with experienced co-driver Jim Scott coming on board as team manager, and a lot more back-up. Snow would become New Zealand's first professional rally technician, and former rival Paul Adams would help with checking pace notes, car set-up, and recces of coming stages.

Meanwhile, in the back of mind, throughout the second half of 1985, there was the Kenyan question. Should I go, or should I stay? Logically it made more sense to get the national rally title under my belt before competing offshore, and getting to Kenya would require a huge effort raising the funds. It was a daunting task, and the easier option was to stay in New Zealand. For there was also Lynne to consider, and the strain going to Africa would put on an already fragile marriage. It wasn't until I bumped into Allan and Colleen Woolf at a social function that I made up my mind. Allan told me that I had to make the most of every opportunity that came my way, and invitations to drive a factory car in the East African Safari didn't come often. This was the first time the offer had been made to a Kiwi driver – I would be mad not to accept.

OTHER PERSPECTIVES:

Allan Woolf – former New Zealand saloon car champion, and long-time rally supporter:

Although I can't remember the exact words, what I probably said to Possum was "You've got to take out of today what you can". It's one of my favourite sayings. Not that Possum ever needed any encouragement to go and drive in a rally. He was, and still is, the most enthusiastic driver I know in the sport. Some years earlier, when my son John was making an impact in the USA, he was asked by a reporter if there were many drivers like him back in New Zealand. His answer was "boatloads", but I'll bet he had a picture of Possum in his mind when he said it.

It was all well and good for me to say such a thing to Possum, but he still had to go out there and do it. I have the greatest admiration for his achievements, yet what I admire most is that he's still the same person that I met all those years ago. His successes haven't changed him. For me that's why so many people can relate to Possum. There's still a touch of the country lad from Meremere about him. You respect the things he says because of that, and it's what makes him so good in any PR role. When I bumped into Possum once at Sydney airport, he started singing the praises of Subarus. It wasn't like he had to talk to me about them, or anything like that, but his enthusiasm for the cars was infectious. That meeting is the main reason a couple of geriatrics like Colleen and I drive around in a Subaru STi Impreza today.

Paul Adams – former New Zealand Rally Champion:
When I joined the Subaru Motorsports Group at the end of 1985, I suddenly understood why Possum would leave our Group A Corolla GT behind on the straights, and we'd catch him on the tighter stages. The RX Turbo had great stability in a straight line, but it kept wanting to go in a straight line compared with the rear-drive Toyota. Four-wheel-drive cars weren't what they are today back then, and we had a misconception that the Subaru was the better car through the corners. It wasn't until I drove it that I had a better understanding of what Possum achieved with that car. He certainly won more battles than he lost. And the closer the win, the more Possum enjoyed it.

In the Southland rally, where Possum scored Subaru's first overall win, we'd both sussed how to deal with the fog and ice. We set our lights lower than the other competitors and drove on dip, where they let their lights blind them. Consequently we could see where we were going, and they couldn't. It's an obvious thing to do these days, but everyone was a greenhorn back then. It was still a tricky rally though. We'd be flat out in fifth, and the revs would suddenly rise. You knew then that you'd just hit a big patch of black ice.

Snow Mooney – ace rally technician:

The race between the crews to get to the best position in service parks was just as fierce as the battles between the drivers on the stages. We'd often arrive with the brakes of the Transit van on fire!

It was during one of these battles that I rolled the van in forest near Rotorua in 1983. It was dark, and I was following the power lines for an indication of where the road was going. They went straight, while the road suddenly turned left, then right, and the inevitable happened. The gear was quickly loaded into a rival team's truck, as everyone helped out everyone else in those days. I was taken to hospital for observation after concussion, but checked out the next day because I didn't want to miss the end of the rally. My parents drove down and picked me up, and we caught up with the team as quickly as we could.

When the car overheated in the 1985 Hella Lights event, we all felt sorry for Possum. His determination to win swept the team along on a wave of dedication and enthusiasm. We'd willingly jump into a mud puddle in the pouring rain, and wallow around in six inches of freezing cold water beneath the car to fix something if it would get him to the finish line. When the motor expired in the Hella Lights, the circumstances were out of our control, and we felt helpless to do anything about it. There was quite a drinking session amongst the boys that night.

ON SAFARI

The 4500-km Safari itself was daunting enough, let alone the money mountain we had to climb to get there. I would be going from the smoothest rally roads in New Zealand to the roughest. Judging by the fortunes of entrants in the 1985 Safari, the potholes could swallow cars whole. The 1985 event had broken one of the Subaru team's cars completely in half, and German driver Edwin Weber was within sight of victory when he hit a big one, collapsing the suspension on his Lancia Rallye. Another tripped up Hannu Mikkola's Audi Quattro at flat chat and sent it rolling end-for-end seven times. Then there were the other "welcome to Africa" factors: air so hot some competitors needed to take off their helmets to stay conscious; impenetrable dust; vicious wildlife, and the "matatus" – utes converted into overcrowded buses that share the stage with you. The Safari races on open roads, so that dust you're driving through could be from a ute carrying 25 people at a quarter of the speed of the rallycar. I couldn't wait to get there.

At that time I had a manager, Darryl Sambell. He was an Australian who also looked after the cricket playing Crowe brothers – Martin and Jeff. Darryl told me just to keep on working, and he'd sort out the fund-raising needed to get to

Kenya. Through articles in newspapers like the *New Zealand Herald,* Darryl made sure the whole country knew what was required to get us to Kenya. Yet things were moving slowly, and when Subaru wanted me to go to Japan to finalise the details of the drive, I still didn't know whether we had enough funds to reach the startline. Darryl was picking up a grand here, and a grand there, but the trip didn't fully gel until an organisation called FADE came on board. FADE stood for the Foundation for Alcohol and Drug Education, and was the brain-child of Murray Deaker – then deputy-principal of Takapuna Grammar School, but soon to make a name for himself in New Zealand as a top sports journalist. Deaker saw me as the ideal front-person for FADE. I was involved in an exciting form of motorsport that was capturing the attention of young people, and enjoyed public speaking. FADE made a considerable contribution towards getting us to Kenya, in return for my PR work for them before and after the Safari. Talking to school assemblies about how drugs and too much alcohol hurts anyone's performance in sports as well as life was no great hardship for me, apart from the time I needed to take off work to do it. Once I stood up there, I thoroughly enjoyed every minute.

So we now had the funds to take myself, and two technicians –
Noel Robinson and Snow Mooney – to Kenya, but no co-driver.
Michael Eggleton was starting a new business and couldn't
afford to take five weeks off to do the Safari. At first we
contemplated using a Kenyan co-driver to take his place, but
settled instead for someone who was a proven performer on
the New Zealand scene. Mike Fletcher, from Christchurch, fitted
the bill, having competed in the Rally of New Zealand with
Timaru driver Carl Rabbidge in a Group A Nissan Bluebird
Turbo. He heard we looking for a replacement, and said he would
go to Kenya as some sort of high-speed holiday.

Thanks to sponsorship from Alpine car audio systems, *Auckland
Star* motoring journalist John Coker could come along later as well.
He'd go on to generate around 10,000 column inches of coverage
in New Zealand newspapers, and help raise the profile of the team's
efforts there, putting the event firmly on the map back home.

Going to Tokyo to finalise the details was like a trip to Mars for me.
It was the first time I'd been outside New Zealand, and I couldn't
believe the number of people crowding the streets and subway

stations. Fuji Heavy Industries, Subaru's parent corporation, has its head office in Shinjuku, home of the busiest subway station in the world. Three million people pass through there every day. When I visited in early 1986, that was the entire population of New Zealand. I had never seen so many people in my life.

The food also took me by surprise. I remember staring at a plate of raw fish, thinking "Well, it hasn't killed them, so go ahead and eat it." I love Japanese food now, but back then I was more used to simpler fare. The culture, so based on respect and status, was also hard to get used to. New Zealand is such a classless society, and understanding how the Japanese do things was hard for someone born on a farm in Meremere.

Fortunately, Yoshio Takaoka, the Subaru team manager, was good at explaining things for me. I was definitely a fish out of water, and Yoshio understood that. He had been educated in the United States, and knew the difficulties I would have with the business culture in Japan. One day he took out a red matchbox, and said "You are driving in a Japanese team now, and I'm the boss. Now if I say this matchbox is white, then it is white, end of story."

It took many months for the penny to drop on what he said, for it to gel into some way of dealing successfully with the Japanese. My interpretation was this: if I wanted something done, then I had to go straight to the top, and have a quiet word with the boss. I'd sort out the issue with him discreetly without anyone else knowing. The boss would then announce the change at the next team meeting. That way you give him the chance to explain the change to the team, and he retains his full authority. To bring up the issue at the meeting, and be critical of the way things were being done in a more open way, was definitely the wrong way to do business with the Japanese. You had to be careful not to reduce what Maori people would call the "mana" of the man in charge. You had to let him have full authority in every decision, otherwise he'd lose face.

It was hard for a head-strong, straight-talking Kiwi to understand this at first. Fortunately, guys like Mike Kirkland, his 1985 co-driver Mike Doughty, and Frank Tundo, helped smooth my entry into the team. They had been dealing with the Japanese for longer, and had a better handle on the rules of engagement.

Japan wasn't the only place that would give me culture shock that year. We travelled to Kenya via Muscat and London, and when passing through Muscat we were herded towards the transit lounge by some goon with a machine gun. At Heathrow, we had about a day to wait for our flight to Kenya, and despite our heavy bags we decided to take the subway into town to look at the sights. I was expecting England to be like something out of the TV series *Coronation Street*, but two stations from Heathrow, it seemed there wasn't an English-speaker on the train.

I began to wonder, in my jet-lagged stupor, whether I was in England at all. The conversation I was hearing made it far more likely that I'd landed in the West Indies.

It was freezing cold in London that February day, and while I was looking at Buckingham Palace, someone came up and said: "You've got a nice accent". My immediate thought was "I haven't got an accent". Then the penny dropped that I was the foreigner in this land. By the time I got on the plane to Nairobi, I was so stuffed that I fell asleep before the plane left the runway.

I woke up in stinking-hot Nairobi. Fortunately, Mike Kirkland was there to meet us and had already tipped us off about entering the country. We had to declare any foreign currency we were carrying in those days, and the customs people wanted us to exchange it with the local currency with them at exorbitant rates. It was the first time I'd encountered corruption. In New Zealand such a practice would be a huge scandal, but in Kenya it was just part of the culture. The whole system was corrupt to the core. We soon learned, as a team, that anything could be bought. It was just a matter of negotiating the price. If they thought you were American then the price would be double, so we quickly learned that declaring our country of origin was an automatic 50 percent discount. Then you'd chop it down another 25 percent, before grinding them down some more. After a week I began to enjoy the haggling.

It took about the same time to get used to the altitude. Nairobi is six thousand feet above sea level, and the first time I ran around the block from the Pan African hotel, it felt like my heart was coming out of my mouth. I thought the flights had really knocked my fitness until I realised it was the altitude. I can see why athletes train in high places, for by a week I was running as strongly as ever. Not so the car. When we started doing reconnaissance for the rally it felt gutless and slow, but altitude was the problem more than the slight motor detune to ensure the engine would last the distance. Some of the Safari's stages are 10,000 feet above sea level. If it was held in New Zealand, that's equivalent to a stage at the top of the Tasman glacier on Mount Cook!

The Pan African was our second choice of hotel. It wasn't the Hilton by any means, but at least the sheets were clean. The first hotel we were booked into was the biggest dog I ever saw, and had just as many fleas. The bed moved with every little sound, and you wouldn't even lie on the floor. Later we moved out of the Pan African, and stayed at Lynn Tundo's Mum's place. Frank had a farm of about 15,000 acres that he leased near Nairobi, and had built a house for his mother-in-law there. It was a fantastic place, and I'll remember all my life how good it felt to wake up there, and their hospitality. When the recce schedule took us near Mombasa, we stayed at Mike Kirkland's place down there. My Kenyan Subaru teammates realised that we were doing the event on a shoestring, and were quick to give us their support. Kenya was, and still is, the most amazing place I've been so far. To stand on top of the Rift Valley and look down on Africa's version of the Grand Canyon is something everyone should do in their lifetime. And the people that get behind the rally were amazing too. The preparation for the event was a lot of work, but it was conducted in a very social atmosphere. They liked to play hard, and party hard afterward. That's what made the 1986 East African Safari so worthwhile. We were so used to doing our own thing.

Getting biffed into something like the Safari made me realise that the job of a professional rally driver was a lot harder than I thought. The saving grace was the support of the Kenyans. Bloody excellent people like Frank, Mike, and their co-drivers Robyn Nixon and Quentin Thompson. Outside the Subaru team there were guys like Shekhar Mehta and Vic Preston – hired Kenyan guns for the factory Peugeot and Lancia Group B teams, but still extending a warm welcome to the Kiwis they'd met on the Rally of New Zealand. The Kenyan drivers helped me read the terrain and the lie of the land. It wasn't like New Zealand where there's a motel every 50 kilometres or so. Sometimes you'd drive 600 kilometres in a day on a recce, because that was the distance to the next place to stay. The other difference was the speed. This wasn't just checking the notes. It was practice. As John Coker wrote in the *Auckland Star*: "Driving is of such a poor standard in Kenya that the rally drivers can't set a bad example". We didn't drive flat out, but sure got a feel of what we were up for in a proper factory rallycar.

Mike Kirkland made sure of that. On the first day, we were about 100 kilometres into the recce, the three cars and their co-drivers linked by radio. I came up to an intersection and found Mike waiting for me.

"You're going to have to pull your finger out," he said, "if we're to get there before dark."

He had been waiting for us for half an hour. Kirkland wasn't one for flowery speeches, and I knew we had to get a whole lot faster in a hurry, but it was so difficult with just a route book full of mistakes for guidance. It was bloody hard work, not knowing when to keep it flat out, and when to back off and avoid a big washout. Not that you could record the washout in the pace notes, because it would be in a different place come the time of the rally. Rain brought constant change to the driving conditions. Once we went over a river crossing that was little more than a trickle. Frank arrived at the ford 10 minutes later and found the water seven feet deep. He had to wait for the flash flood to recede before continuing. The water disappeared just as fast as it arrived, as he knew it would. This was the reason Kenyan drivers were so much in demand by the factory teams for the Safari – they knew best how to cope with the conditions.

By 1985 there had been 33 Safaris, and in 27 of those years, a Kenyan won on the back of their local knowledge. They knew where they were going, and we were starting from scratch. On the other side of the ledger, the Japanese knew we Kiwis were coming from the smoothest international rally of the calendar to the roughest, and were hoping against hope that we wouldn't destroy the car in the first 100 kilometres. We didn't.

But we got Kirkland back all the same. We were in a stage that was 180 kilometres long, through grass that was higher than the roof of the car. It was incredibly hard work navigating through the grass, and driving at a decent pace, but I knew we were ahead. So I faked an off, and we were going through the grass calling on the radio that we couldn't get back on the road because we might collide with Mike coming up behind us. He radioed in to say that he was further back than we thought. "Surely you can't be that late," I said on the radio with a wry smile.

Most of the time, though, they'd stop to have a smoke, while Mike and I caught up. They had pace notes from several years earlier, while we were always stopping to write up a new set. One time, we were in the Taita Hills, dodging these strange looking rocks. There was one I couldn't dodge, yet the car didn't feel a thing, as the rock seemed to explode under its wheels. When we caught up with Mike Kirkland and Frank, they said "Did you miss all the rocks?"

I said "No, we hit one, but it was as soft as shit."

"Well it was shit," said Frank, "Elephant shit."

They had a good laugh at that one. They were always taking the piss – at us, themselves, the ever-changing conditions. One part of Kenya had this "black cotton soil", and when it's dry you just drive over it. But if it rains, it turns into black cottonwool, and just bogs the car. Next thing you know the car's sitting on its diffs in the stuff. I soon learned to follow Kirkland's advice, and keep an eye on the surrounding hills for rain. I'd never seen rain like it. The drops were as big as your fist, and there wasn't a windscreen wiper that could deal with them. It would teem down an inch of rainfall every minute. One time, we'd just crossed a bridge, and were having a bit of a break, when Kirkland started yelling to get the cars away from the water. He'd spotted it raining in the hills, and sure enough, the flash flood arrived minutes later. In next to no time the bridge was under three feet of water.

It took us eight days to do the first recce of a 4200 kilometres course that we'd cover in five days during the Safari itself. Then I was crook for three days with an intense, feverish dose of diarrhoea. The team called the doctor in, but I was out for the count. So I missed some of the second phase of the recce, where you check whether the notes that you made on the first round are right. Although I never had any more medical dramas in Kenya, I never got to do the entire course twice.

It wasn't quite gelling with Mike Fletcher at first. It made me realise just how good Michael Eggleton was as a co-driver. It was worth putting up with a smelly car to have someone of his calibre. By comparison, Mike Fletcher lacked experience, and I found his calls often came too late. We sorted out the timing in a chat immediately after we ran off the road one time too many, but to me it was obvious that New Zealanders, in general, had been held back by the lack of pace notes in their home rallies for so long. This was only the third rally with pace notes for both of us. Mike did take what I said to heart, and applied himself to the task, but calling this rally was hard enough for a co-driver on his 10th Safari, let alone his first. He got callouses on his fingers from writing so many notes. At the end of the recces, he had filled 17 notebooks with notes – 850 pages in all. So he was trying the best he could. And he sure came in handy at times, such as when the right rear suspension broke. Mike sat on the left side of the bonnet to keep that wheel-less corner of the car in the air while the Subaru limped home on three wheels. That was three and a half weeks into a six-week recce of the course. We were near Lake Victoria when a trailing arm snapped and tore the right-rear wheel, hub and brakes from the car. With Mike's weight balancing the car, we drove for 20 kilometres on three wheels to higher ground so we could call up the boys on the radio. When we stopped, Masai tribespeople appeared from nowhere and surrounded the car. They treated us like rock stars.

It was going to take ages for Snow and Noel to get there, and we were starving. The Masai gave us some hard-boiled eggs to eat – so hard-boiled they were like crunching rocks. Nearby, an ox carcass hung from a tree. They made a fire, and cut strips of meat off the carcass and cooked it for us. I don't know how long it had been hanging in the tree, but it sure tasted good. When the boys finally arrived, they fixed the car, and we eventually got to bed at three in the morning. We were up three hours later at six to start the recce again.

The rear end was one of the issues with the RX Turbo. If we settled for suspension settings that were too soft, the rough roads just pounded everything to bits. If we set up the car too hard to stop it bottoming out, the handling suffered, and it just wanted to swap ends all the time. The RX needed more wheel travel before we could find a happy compromise for the Safari. We just had to make do with what we had, and erred on the soft side to keep the car on the road, while hoping we could keep replacing suspension parts before they wore out.

For the second recce of the course, Mike Fletcher and I were on our own. We were way out the back of beyond when we wrecked the recce car. We hit two goats at 180 km/h, and they made a hell of a mess. It happened at 10.30 am in the morning, and we were out of radio range. We sat in the car for another five hours, fretting about our smashed windscreen, and the possibility that the smell of goat's blood might attract lions. It was 4 pm before another vehicle came along – a truck with no windows in it, and a load of Africans in the back. We hooked up the car to the truck and got it towed to the main road. Five hours later we finally reached the road. There was a barrier there and I told this guy standing by it to guard the car.

"Take anything off it, and we'll hunt you down and kill you," I threatened, "however, if nothing is missing when we come back, you'll be rewarded."

It might sound cruel and colonial these days, but Mike and Frank had taught me that gross threats coupled with the promise of rich rewards was the best way to get things done in Kenya. We all carried plenty of money in small denominations for times of need. The Safari term for it was "push money." It was what you used when you had an off, and needed help to get the car back on the course. During the Safari, squads of tribespeople stake out the corners likely to catch a driver out, usually with a rope handy, in the hope of making a little money. They're not above building their own obstacles in the road to cause a crash either, or tossing the odd rock through the windscreen.

Through Lynn Tundo's landline, I finally got hold of Noel and Snow to tell them where to find the car, and about the two goat carcasses growing out of the radiator. They dropped their drinks to start the rescue mission while Mike and I rode back in the truck.

I doubt if anyone on the back had had a bath in the last year or so. We finally got to bed sometime around five in the morning.

Next day, the Japanese were unhappy about all the damage we were wreaking on the recce car, but it was all part of figuring out just how hard we could go in the RX Turbo. The lack of suspension travel meant the rear shocks got seriously hot, so hot the skin would lift off your hands if you touched them. When they got this hot, the damping would go away, and the car would "pogo" all over the place. We needed to know what the car was like in rally conditions, but Takaoka was getting uptight about all the damage on the recce car, and all the bits we were using.

Not that any of that was in my mind when the Safari finally started. We were seeded 15th, and going over the start ramp was a memory I'll always treasure. There was something about the Safari that year – the people we met and got to know better, and the country and all its wild beauty. It will always be a special place for me. It was such a special feeling going over the ramp in my first international rally outside New Zealand. I felt I had gained new respect from within the World Rally Championship community. We followed lots of international rally stars onto those dusty, rough, and treacherous roads that day. The race up front in Group B would be between two-time Safari winner Bjorn Waldegard in a Toyota Celica TC, and Juha Kankkunen in the fire-spitting Peugeot 205 T16. They would hit speeds approaching 250 km/h on the famous "Pipeline" – a pedal-to-the-metal straight that lasted 42 kilometres. This contrasted sharply with the tight stage through the Taita Hills, where Mike would rip through 50 pages of pace notes in just 100 kilometres of road. The Peugeot team had been told to "win at all costs", and while Toyota weren't such a threat to them in the World Championship, a strong Lancia team of Markku Alen, Massimo Biasson, and Vic Preston was. Then there was the dark horse of the event, Shekhar Mehta in a Nissan 240RS (despite his role as Kenya's Subaru importer). The Group A battle was played out between our Subarus and a strong VW Golf GTi factory contingent with 1985 Safari near-winner Edwin Weber as lead driver.

I settled straight into a good rhythm, and we immediately started moving up the field. When we got to the Taita Hills that night, Mike and I were third fastest on some stages. We were going real good, and were up to fifth place at one point. Then Takaoka came on the radio to give us the hard word:

"You are going too fast," he said, "you must slow down otherwise you'll break the car."

So slow down we did, and we just got hammered. It's hard to find your rhythm again after such a call. You may be losing a few seconds a kilometre, but when you're talking about stages that are 180 kilometres long, that quickly adds up to quite a deficit. We went from 10 minutes in front of the Group A field to 15 minutes behind the leading Group A car. We tried to make it up again and finished the first day of the Safari in ninth place overall. We were the second Group A car home, three minutes behind Mike Kirkland, and 10 in front of Weber.

On the second day, the pace notes took us up the Rift Valley into the areas where we'd experienced the flash floods. I was trying to use Mike Kirkland as a guide to the speed we should be driving. I'd finish the stages in a similar time to him, yet I felt I had plenty of speed left. There were times when he'd be faster than me, and others when he'd be slower, so it was all a bit erratic and hit-and-miss as we battled for the Group A lead. Due to a lack of experience in the Safari, it's fair to say that I was harder on the car than him. We got past him and up to fourth overall at one stage, but slipped back to sixth overall with a puncture. Then disaster struck. We went through a big mud puddle, then round a bend. The car hit a rock and one of the front wheel hubs broke. Bruce Field, who we'd just passed, was quickly on the scene in the team's chase car. We ripped into it, changing the damaged hub for one of his in 16 minutes. Then we jumped back in the car, and I was so pissed off at losing the time, that I blew it. I took off too hard. We came around a corner a few kilometres further on to find this huge washout staring at us. I hit the brakes hard as the second front wheel hub collapsed, the wheel jammed under the guard, dug in, and rolled the car over a couple of times. We radioed back to Bruce that we'd need his other hub, and starting pulling the damaged car apart. By the time we waited for the second chase car to bring the wheel hub up to us, and got the car repaired, it was too late. We were over time arriving for the end of the stage, and out of the Safari.

When we got back to base, the Japanese guys started giving us a hard time about the car. It was pretty knocked about, and they thought I'd screwed up, while I couldn't decide whether I had or not at the time. I was so pissed off, I decided work was the only cure. So I got stuck into the servicing of Frank's and Mike's cars. Frank's rear shocks were gone halfway through a section, so Poko, a big Japanese guy, and I formed a plan to change them. We got organised, sorted out which bolts each of us would attack, and got cracking as soon as Frank slewed to a stop. The job took us a minute and a half. Frank, sitting in the car, was back on the ground so soon he thought the jack was broken. He had this look of disbelief on his face when we screamed at him to go. He went on to finish seventh overall and second in Group A. Mike finished sixth and first in Group A. Waldegard won the overall prize. Mike Fletcher and I picked up a special award for the most meritorious performance of the Safari. We won an elephant trophy each, and 3000 Kenyan shillings (around $NZ350). It was quite a lot of money at the time, but not as much as I would have won if I'd finished the Safari. The local bookmakers were offering odds of 300-to-1 on my reaching the finish.

So Takaoka-san was a happier man come the end of the Safari with his Group A success. He apologised humbly to Mike and I for the collapse of the front hubs. The team had used our car to practise their front suspension strut changes, and jamming wedges into the top of hubs to take the tension off the springs many times over had weakened them and caused cracks. Both had failed within a couple of kilometres on the longest section of the Safari towards the end of the second day. We weren't to blame, and Mike and I left Kenya with clear consciences.

OTHER PERSPECTIVES:

Noel Robinson – legendary engine lifter:

Snow and I spent six weeks in Kenya, looking after Possum and Mike. We soon learned how to order a cold beer in Swahili. If you ordered in English, you wouldn't get a cold one.

One night, we were sitting back after a hard day, having a couple of cold ones, when Possum rang up to say that he had a couple of goats "growing out of the radiator." So we dropped the beers, borrowed Shekhar Mehta's Land Cruiser and a tow-rope, and headed out there. It was about 9.30 pm when we left, and around one in the morning when we finally found the car. There was a bloke looking after it, and he was scared stiff. I dunno if it was something Possum had said to him, or whether it was the threat of lions. There was blood and guts all over the car, and someone had thrown a rock through the windscreen. I drew the short straw, and had to sit in the smashed-up Subaru all the way back to base. Snow kept telling me it was lion country just to make me feel comfortable. We eventually got back at 6 am – just in time to start work again.

In the Subaru camp, Snow and I quickly became known as the "engine lifters". It took eight of the Japanese mechanics to get the engine out of the car with a block and tackle, and they were highly impressed when Snow and I could do it without lifting equipment. Without the top end fitted, we could walk around the workshop carrying an engine by ourselves. If they wanted an engine put on a bench, they'd politely ask me to do it for them. It may have killed our backs at the time, but we weren't going to let them know that. One time a Japanese TV crew paid the team a visit, and there was footage of this bloke from Pukekohe lugging this Subaru engine around the workshop on the news.

John Coker – Sports Journalist:
I arrived in Kenya three days before the rally began to cover Possum and Mike's Safari debut. I was there at Possum's request, and part of his commitment to FADE – who wanted to generate plenty of press about their front-person. Possum also realised early just how important a tool the media was for furthering his career. He certainly made the job easy, with his colourful speech and happy-go-lucky personality. It certainly made a change from covering sports-people who talked in grunts and nods.

Covering the Safari was an adventure I'll never forget. It sometimes involved getting into a clapped-out hire car, driving into the bush over those rough roads for four hours to get a ten-minute interview, then driving four hours back again to the nearest place where I could file the story. I'd pay the Kenyan telex operators, then stand over them to make sure they sent the thing. All the other journalists were from Europe, and their reports weren't so time-critical. The reports went on to the New Zealand Press Association, and were picked up by most of the nation's newspapers. For a week, it felt like the whole country was keen to know how Possum was getting on.

SKY, GROUND, SKY

Snow Mooney, Noel Robinson and I returned to New Zealand via England, staying at Jonathan Ashman's house in London. We never realised how much we had missed the food we were used to until we went to a pub down by the Thames, and had a huge feed of sausages, baked beans, and eggs. It tasted sensational after nearly two months in Kenya. Our stomachs enjoyed a welcome return to Western food. We'd all lost weight on the Safari, and the heat and the hard work had sucked kilograms from our bodies.

Coming back home jolted me back to everyday routines. The days on the Safari, living the life of the jet-setting professional rally driver, seemed like a dream. In Kenya, I was far removed from the daily realities of my life, and fully focused on one thing – the race. Returning to Pukekohe meant returning to the daily challenges, and there were some things I really didn't want to face – the slow corrosion of my marriage, and the need to work hard to get to the next rally.

The relationship between Lynne and I had started out positively enough, and Mum and Dad treated her like another daughter, but you don't really know someone until you live together. After first six months of our marriage I'd realised that it might not last, but I was still committed to making it work. The Safari had really exposed the cracks in our fragile partnership. We were very different people. She had things that she wanted to do, and they had nothing in common with the things that I wanted to do. With two people heading in such different directions, it's only a matter of time before they part to get on with what they want to achieve in life. It would take another year for our marriage to slowly unravel.

I arrived home on a Tuesday night, and went straight into work on Wednesday morning. Just off the plane from the greatest adventure of my life to selling lights and electrical parts for Lucas. I was their top-selling sales rep, making 160 calls in the South Auckland region a week. Wayne Hopkins was the branch manager, and he knew that I'd need roughly 17 weeks off a year to pursue my motorsport career. As he used to do my run before me, he could step into my shoes anytime I was away. I'm sure it pissed him off that he had to keep going back out on the road, but it sure worked out well for me.

Time away from work was one of the reasons I stopped driving trucks for Jim and John Evans after three and a half years. They were really good guys to work for, and I couldn't have asked for better bosses, but I felt my need for time off was getting in the way of what they wanted to achieve. It was also bloody hard work, and I earned every cent. On my first day there I had to deliver 20 tonnes of cement in a truck and trailer, and unload it by myself, bag by bag. It took all day. The good part was that the physical part of the job kept me fit, although I wasn't really thinking about my race fitness back then. That became more of an issue when I moved to a less physical job.

Becoming a sales rep gave me a better understanding of how to sell myself to sponsors, but selling parts seemed relatively easy compared with signing up potential sponsors. Both rely on building relationships, but it takes a lot less negotiation when the customer really needs the parts you're selling him. Rallying isn't a sport with any guarantees. It's not like you can say to the sponsor that you'll get so many minutes of TV exposure on TV One at such and such a time. You've got to get them to believe in you, you've got to get them keen to be involved as part of your team. Finding enough money to get to the start-line has always been a shit-fight. It still is today.

So it was a bit perplexing to return from Kenya to find Subaru New Zealand reassessing its commitment to motorsport. Motor

Holdings had sold the distribution rights to the Giltrap Group, and the new management of Adam Poulopoulos and Jack Rae were still making up their minds about the local branch of the Subaru Motorsports Group. We certainly had some talented people on board in the form of Paul Adams and Jim Scott, my experienced co-driver for the season. Jim had competed in the World Rally Championship, calling the notes for Ari Vatanen. But good support doesn't come cheap, and our national rally championship effort that year was to be a compete-when-we-can-afford-it exercise. Darryl Sambell was finding money to keep us going, and the Subaru dealer network stumped up to fill in for the loss of distributor support for a while. They could see the value in what we were doing.

So the biggest crash of my career (touch wood) came at what was possibly the worst time. We were testing for the Rally of New Zealand up in the Kaukapakapa Forest. Paul Adams did some of the first runs in the car, and warned me about the tyres. "They suddenly go off," he said. But the problem wasn't the tyres; it was the rear axle. Snow's one moment of glory as a co-driver came to an abrupt end when the stub axle snapped, dug into the ground, and rolled the car through an open gate, and down a hill. It rolled, and kept on rolling – nine times end for end, and almost as many side to side. The impacts pummelled the car into a sardine tin, breaking the alloy roll cage. When the crazy kaleidoscope of sky-ground-sky finally stopped, I heard Snow yell, "Fire!" So I undid the belts and rolled out of the broken front windscreen before the pain and shock set in.

It was a bloody miracle that we both walked away from that crash. We'd never use aluminium in a roll cage again despite the opportunity to save weight. The car was an absolute mess, a complete write-off – or so we thought. My right wrist was feeling second-hand as well. I'd broken the scaphoid bone trying the keep the car on the road. Snow told me he had heard a bang in the back end of the car a split second before the crash. He also told me his one thought immediately prior to this four-wheeled equivalent of a barrel ride over Niagara Falls, was: 'If he saves this one, he's God.'

The RX Turbo we mashed was one Frank Tundo was due to drive in the Rally of New Zealand. We sent photos of the crashed car to the Subaru Motorsports Group in Japan to keep them informed of this new development. They faxed back to say that it looked like the car was scrap metal, and unrepairable. Once again we were in deep shit for being hard on the gear. But the boys really got stuck into the wreck, and by the time Frank arrived for the rally, the car looked like nothing had happened to it. Frank went on to finish the job by violently rolling it out of the rally. That poor old RX Turbo had finally had its day.

It was an unforgettable Rally of New Zealand for the Subaru team. The battle for Group A honours was a fierce one at first. After Frank's roll on the first day, Mike Kirkland and I were left to fend off strong challenges from the Volkswagen Golf GTi of Kenneth Eriksson, and the newly developed 4wd Mazda 323 Turbo of Rod Millen. As a backdrop to the Group A battle, there was the recent decision by the FIA in Paris to ban Group B cars at the end of the season. The more production-based cars were to become rallying's premier class in 1987, and Subaru, VW, and Mazda were keen to begin the new era as hot favourites for World Rally Championship success. My wrist hadn't healed four weeks after the crash. The broken bone was taking its time to knit back together and I was driving with a lightweight plastic cast around it. It took a while to get used to, but with Jim calling the notes we were on the pace, and scrapping with Millen and Eriksson all the way, until the tragedy happened.

Dunlop were looking after our tyres, and their service crew included top tyre engineer Osamu Kobayashi. He was a passenger in the Dunlop truck when it collided with a farmer's vehicle on State Highway 12 near Paparoa in Northland. The farmer was driving an old fire truck, and did a U-turn right in front of the Dunlop truck, fatally injuring Kobayashi. He hung on for another three hours, but died in Whangarei Hospital that night. We got the bad news while competing in the night stages of the rally. There would be no fourth consecutive Group A win in the Rally of New Zealand for me. As a mark of respect for the passing of Dunlop's top technician, the Subaru team withdrew from the event.

While Eriksson eventually subdued Millen to win the Group A crown, our team went to the accident site to pay our respects to Osamu. In Japanese custom we wished him Godspeed by marking the site with flowers, and pouring bottles of his favourite whisky on the accident-scarred road.

The rally didn't do my broken wrist any good, and after another four weeks it still wasn't healing. Driving my sales round didn't help, and x-rays kept confirming that the bone wasn't knitting together. Finally, I went to a health food shop, and bought a product called "Bone Grow". I started taking this stuff, and two weeks later the wrist was perfect. The doctor couldn't believe it. It went from a complete break to fully fixed in a matter of days. I've been a believer in natural healing and homeopathic stuff ever since.

While getting to national rallies in 1986 was a hit-and-miss affair, the Subaru Motorsports Group did allow me to make it to three international rallies. Whenever Mr Takaoka found surplus finds, usually from the domestic publicity budget, he'd use them to get our team to an event. The deal was always that Subaru would take care of the car expenses, and we'd look after the rest. The

Olympus Rally in the state of Washington was a round of the World Rally Championship in 1986, and our last international event of the year. Organiser John Naval waived the entry fee to help get us there. But when Jim, Snow, Richard Syverston, and I arrived in Seattle, there wasn't a lot of money in the team kitty.

Subaru would ship our Rally of New Zealand car to Seattle, but we still needed a place to work, and a recce car. Fortunately, the international rally community came to the rescue. Bjorn Waldegard, his co-driver Fred Gallagher, and Rod Millen helped us get settled and introduced us to Ray, a real hard-case Mazda dealer. We told Ray we needed a car, and he took us to his junkyard where there was a worn-out old Datsun 180B. He loaned it to us for $600, and said we had to fix anything that broke while we had it. He said he'd give us our money back at the end of the loan. I was terrified about the cost of insuring the Datsun, but Ray told us not to worry.

"Just take it," he said. " If you have an accident, and can still run, just get the f— out of there fast, give me a ring, and I'll tell the police that the car's been stolen."

Once we fixed a worn CV joint in the driveshaft, the 180B was a good recce car. We would give it back in better nick than when we first saw it. Despite the rain. Washington is a state famous for its mushrooms, and for good reason. There always seems to be some form of moisture in the air there – fog, drizzle, or plain old rain. There were floods as Jim and I scouted the stages and prepared our pace notes. We were driving through a foot of water on one of them, and these salmon started passing us. They were escaping from a salmon farm nearby. So we put the Datsun's indicator on, and started passing them right back!

Meanwhile, Snow scoured Seattle for a workshop we could use. He found a Subaru and Chevrolet dealer called Ken Parks, and we went into his place to see if he had any spare workshop space we could clutter up. Ken was 65 years old, but didn't look a day over 40. He invited us to stay and have lunch with he and Ellen – his American-Japanese girlfriend. I sensed we were meeting a new team patron in Ken, so I hit him with our proposal. We needed to use his workshop, and we were $5000 under any budget that would allow us to do the rally properly. Ken suddenly got up, and offered his hand.

"My hand is my word," he said. "When the car arrives in the workshop, I'll give you the money."

With Ken's generosity we were set up for the rally. He would become a friend for life from that moment on. But he was a real hard man. His Dad had been a coalminer, and he had built up a 300-car dealership with his bare hands and sheer grit. He owned everything – the cars, buildings, and the prime land they stood on. In World War Two, Ken had been one of the first American soldiers to enter Hiroshima, and most of his friends from that unit had since died from cancer. But the big "C" wouldn't dare mess around with Ken, although it had claimed his wife five years earlier. He told me he still expected her to greet him when he went home at night.

Ken's passion wasn't rallying – it was mushroom hunting in the hills around Seattle. Ellen, a divorcée in her mid-30s, ran the business while he was away. One day, I was sitting in Ken's office – for he let us use that too – and Ellen came in for a chat.

"You need to understand what's going on here," she said. "Ken's never sponsored anybody in his life before. And no one, except myself, has ever been allowed in his office. We can't believe what he's done. He's given you guys full use of his office. Not that there's anything wrong with that – don't get me wrong. We're all happy that you've become like sons to him."

Ken was so much more than a sponsor. He started taking us out to dinner at night once he realised how broke we were. He found out we were going to this place called The King's Table, where you could pay $5, and eat everything. We were going in there every second night, eating ourselves stupid, and then fasting for two days, because that's all we could afford. Ken even took us to one of his "steak and beans" nights for his sales people.

There were two sales shifts at the dealership, as it was open from 6am in the morning to 10pm at night. At the end of each month, Ken would look at the sales figures, and reward the shift with the most sales by giving them steak, while the losing team got beans.

He had a great car collection, including one of the first Cadillacs. He housed them in his own museum, and none of the exhibits had travelled more than 1000 miles. One night we were talking on the lot, and I made a comment about a Z28 Camaro that had just been traded.

"I've always wanted one of those," I said.

He got me the keys, and said, "Here, take it."

The boys and I had a great time that night, cruising the streets of Seattle. We tried to repay Ken somehow. He came and had a look at one of the practice stages, but the weather was atrocious (it wasn't much better for the rally). When one of the guys from Subaru America came up to help us, he told me that there were 200 demo cars coming up for sale. I passed this info on to Ken, and he snapped them up. He was always having trouble finding enough Subaru stock to sell, and this was one small way I could help him out. He on-sold the lot before they even arrived at the dealership, and was stoked. It was the first month he'd ever sold more Subarus than Chevs.

America took a bit of getting used to. We rented this little
apartment next to Ken's dealership. One of the rally organisers
showed up one morning, and said, "I've bought you some
doughnuts for breakfast."

Doughnuts? We nearly chucked at the thought.

Then, there was driving on the right side of the road. Our car
was right-hand-drive, and it was the first time I'd driven in a
country where I'd be sitting closer than Jim to the kerb on the
transport stages.

It hosed down for the rally. On one of the first stages, Jim and I
came to a ford in the road, swollen with flood water.

"That looks a bit deep," I said.

"It sure is," Jim replied. "Look at that."

It was the latest factory Toyota Celica, almost fully submerged,
with just the roof poking above the surface. The Toyota team
would eventually drag out and drain the Celica submarine, but
it was one competitor down for us, as we engaged Rod Millen
in a battle for Group A honours. Up front, the Lancia of Markku
Alen was fighting the Peugeot of Juha Kankkunen not only for
the win, but also for the 1986 World title in the last World Rally
Championship event of the year. It would all end in tears –
Markku won, with Juha second, but there was to be appeal and

counter-appeal over the legitimacy of the winning Lancia before the title was decided in Juha's favour. Meanwhile, Rod Millen was flying over roads he knew like the back of his hand. After years of competing stateside, he rated the Olympus as the best rally in the US, and the fast stages suited the extra speed of his Mazda. We were doing a good job of keeping him in sight until the car coughed to a halt in the middle of a stage. Out of fuel. I cursed the Japanese mechanic responsible, as a dozen spectators gathered round the silent Subaru. One of them, who drove a speedway car, offered to get some race gas from his nearby car. Running both ways, he returned after a few minutes. While he recovered, we flipped the fuel into the car, and were quickly on our way to finish eighth overall and second in Group A to Rod, who finished seventh overall.

Despite the fuel fiasco, it wasn't a bad result. With Group A becoming the premier rally class in 1987, Subaru confirmed that I'd be a starter in three internationals for the year – the Safari, Rally of New Zealand, and the RAC Rally in Great Britain. All three would be with different co-drivers – Kevin Lancaster in Africa, Michael Eggleton at home, and Rodger Freeth in the UK. After cutting all the finger tendons in his hand while helping Neil Allport get their stricken Mazda off a stump at the Olympus, bike champ Rodger couldn't ride motorcycles anymore. He'd become my preferred co-driver instead.

Subaru went full throttle at Kenya, fielding four cars to even up the odds of a successful finish in the Safari. Ari Vatanen drove the lead-car, seeded number one in the new Group A climate. It was huge kudos for a Subaru to be the first car over the start ramp, and a proud moment for the team. The other two cars were for Per Eklund and Frank Tundo. So there were two fast Scandinavians, a Kenyan veteran, and me – a Kiwi apprentice who had done enough the previous year to be given another go. In Nairobi I met Mr Kuze, the Fuji board member who directed Subaru's increased investment in the World Rally Championship. He was the man who held my future in his hands.

When I first started driving for Subaru, the first contact with the Japanese management was through Mr Koseki and Mr Kuroshima. The Subaru Motorsports Group grew from humble beginnings; it was like a club of engineers from the R&D department, and running a rally team was their working holiday. As a higher profile in rally competition began to have a positive effect on sales and brand image, so SMG grew in resources and stature within Subaru. Mr Kuze was the man pulling strings in the boardroom for an increased commitment to rallysport, and that linked his future dreams and aspirations with mine. We both wanted to win the Safari so badly it hurt.

As the fastest Subaru driver the previous year, I certainly had a chance, although it was back to square one with the pace notes.

Kevin would do a reasonable job, but he had a hard time adapting to the climate and the food. Looking back, it was a mistake to take a person I hadn't used before to a big endurance event like the Safari. Kevin did OK, but the Safari demands more than that. Because of his lack of experience with pace notes, we clicked better out of the car than in it. Jim would have done a better job of plotting and calling the course, but he was getting on in years. A Safari sucks around four or five kilograms of weight from your body, and the most physically demanding rally of them all would have knocked Jim around too much.

During recon, Per, Frank, and I sussed out the stages together, while Ari did his own thing. Frank would give his co-driver Quentin Thompson a real hard time, but Quentin got him back. We did this real rough section, and Frank changed all his notes from the previous year. The big potholes – and we're talking African-sized potholes – had migrated to the other side of the road, and someone had driven a huge truck through in the wet, scouring out deep ruts. So there were quite a few changes to make. At the end of the stage, Frank turned to Quentin and said, "Did you get all that?"

"No, I forgot my pencil," said Quentin , straight-faced.

At night, Frank told us about farming in Kenya, and dealing with tractor blow-ups. His workers wouldn't notice the engines overheating, so he extended the radiator overflow pipes to point at their feet, telling them to stop and switch off if they ever felt their feet getting hot. Trouble was, the barefooted workers had feet as tough as nails – they kept on driving the boiling tractors to their deaths. So Frank redirected the pipes to point at their faces. There were no further blow-ups, but Frank did get a visit from the African Affairs people.

Team leader Mr Takaoka called the shots from the plane during the rally. There were two major issues to deal with – tyres and rear diffs. I came out with all four wheels spinning, setting third fastest time on some of the early stages, behind Bjorn Waldegard's Toyota and Hannu Mikkola's Audi. Then, the diff broke, near a service, but it took the Japanese mechanics 35 minutes to fix it. Snow Mooney and Noel Robinson weren't with me that year, and we missed them. I was so annoyed that it took the factory guys that long. Instead of starting third the next day, we were down the field, choking on the dust of slower cars as we fought hard to get that half-hour back.

There was some mistake with the batch of Bridgestone tyres we used in the rally. Ari got 16 punctures during the event, and I got 11. One time, at one of the controls, Ari spotted the top Bridgestone technician. He grabbed the guy by the shoulders, stared him in the eye with the cold-steel gaze of anger only a Finn is capable of, and said: "Your tyres aren't even good for lighting fires."

He had changed three punctures that stage.

The regular deflations made it hard to stay cool. I was driving in the dust of a Daihatsu, or some other bloody slow thing, and got caught out by a sharp corner. The back wheel went over the edge of the road, and the impact tore the trailing arm of the rear suspension out. We had to muck around fixing that for ages, because we were in the middle of the stage, far from our backup. For the first four days of the five-day event our score for day one was: broke diff; day two: broke trailing arm; day three: third fastest; day four: third fastest; every day: punctures. So going into the last day, we were mounting a pretty decent fight back, blowouts be damned.

Then, the rear diff broke again, this time miles from nowhere. So I jacked up the car, removed the rear diff and axles, and hurled them angrily into the drain. We were four stages from the finish, and I was determined to finish in front-wheel-drive. However Takaoka insisted the rear diff be reinstalled at the next service, losing more time. We finished a dismal 11th, when it could have so easily been fifth.

That Safari was a life-changing event, not because of what happened in a dramatic race, but what happened at one of the services. It was early in the morning. Although the air was cool, I was hot and thirsty from driving hard. I asked for some water and from our support team an attractive young blonde appeared and offered me some. She looked gorgeous in the Kilimanjaro dawn. Her name was Peggy, and she was the daughter of a missionary pilot from Florida. We chatted until the car was ready. The conversation flowed, and we glanced at the mountain every time the eye contact made it obvious where things were heading.

At the post-rally celebrations, she came storming up to me and asked: "Do you dance as well you drive?"

There was only one answer.

"Of course," I said. And I led the future mother of my children to the dance floor.

My marriage with Lynne was already buggered when I met Peggy, so dancing the night away with this vibrant, African-born American woman was no big issue. Nor was spending my last three days in Kenya with her. I told her about Lynne, and she said I should sort things out before we took things further. We exchanged addresses and promised to stay in contact.

Lynne had also met someone else while I was away. We both realised it was time to separate, and get on with our lives. So I agreed to buy her half of the house, and went on a bit of a holiday while she moved out. Mum and Dad were quite upset about it. Their generation simply didn't do things like that, and they worried about the effect of the split on my meagre finances.

I never knew when I'd see Peggy again, but I did write and send her some bits and pieces that Christmas – including newspaper clippings about my success in New Zealand.

With Subaru New Zealand getting involved in the national rally championship again, we were putting in some good performances at home, but it was the international rally that really put us on the map. The AWA-Clarion Rally of New Zealand was downgraded to just being a round of the World Drivers' championship that year, and a lot of the leading factory teams stayed at home. Without the incentive of manufacturers' championship points, many team managers saved their powder for other rounds, but there were still the factory Volkswagen Golf GTis to beat, and the wily 1984 world champion – Stig Blomqvist. Then there were the top locals – Ray Smith, Tony Teesdale, and Neil Allport in Mazda 323 turbos, and Paddy Davidson in a Nissan.

Like all rallies, it was a war of attrition. When Blomqvist dropped out on the seventh stage of the rally, Ray Wilson became the fastest driver on the next two stages, before retiring in a cloud of oil smoke. Michael Eggleton and I finished in third place on the first day, 45 seconds behind the leader – Austrian privateer Franz Whittmann in a Lancia Delta HF. Two battles developed on the second day – Whittmann fought over first place with Kenneth Eriksson (VW Golf GTi), while Neil Allport and I battled for third, and the honour of being the first New Zealand driver. Neil had overhauled me on the first day before losing six minutes with a puncture. On the second day I was often faster than second-placed Eriksson, but a puncture dropped us back by one minute, and back into Allport's clutches. Neil's Mazda blew a differential that evening, allowing us to ease up on the third day and cruise home in third place.

It would be Subaru's best-ever finish in a round of the World Rally Championship, and I winced when the RX Turbo smacked into a rock on one of the last stages. Fortunately the car took the hit in its stride, and we made the finish without further dramas. It sure wouldn't have pleased Mr Kuze if I'd broken the car within sight of the finish.

With no special stages on the fourth day, the team celebrated twice over – on the night of the third day, and at the official finish in Auckland. Eriksson was annoyed that the last day was just a transport day, as he reckoned another four stages would have given him the opportunity to reel in the 47-second gap to Whittmann's Lancia. I was rapt to finish eight minutes behind Eriksson. Third place earned me A-seeding status, giving me automatic entry into any future World Rally Championship event. It also locked down the deal to do the RAC Rally in November.

Michael couldn't come with me, so I rang Rodger Freeth to see if he was interested.

"There's no money to speak of, but are you still interested in giving it a crack?" I asked.

He took all of a couple of seconds to say yes. Rodger had plenty of co-driving experience, usually calling the notes for Neil Allport. As a professor of astrophysics, he brought a scientific approach to co-driving, and even developed one of the first pace-noting machines. At the Rally of New Zealand, I checked his machine's notes against our notes, and they weren't that different.

Mr Kuze got us to the RAC with the help of Subaru's Swiss distributor. Freddy Kestler was the team manager, and I stayed at Freddy's house in a village near Zurich to help prepare the car with technicians Roland Baumann and Soren Jacobsson. One day we needed to pick up some Bilstein shocks from the factory up near Cologne, so I found myself on the autobahn at 6.30 am, bound for the Bilstein factory in a new RX Turbo Coupe. It was one of the best driving experiences of my life. At first I drove flat-out – 225 km/h – but quickly knocked it back to 210 km/h when I realised that the lower cruising speed dramatically improved fuel consumption. Despite missing a turn-off, and covering an extra 360 kilometres, I was back at our base by 8 pm that night. When I pulled up, the trip meter recorded that I'd travelled 1760 kilometres that day. It staggered me to think that I'd driven an equivalent distance to the entire length of

New Zealand in thirteen and a half hours, but Germany's
network of unrestricted motorways make such feats possible.

Closer to the rally, we shipped the car to the United Kingdom,
and Rodger flew in. The RAC was one of the few World Rally
Championship events that didn't allow pace notes at that stage,
and most teams got a feel for the stages by going over
topographic maps with a magnifying "pot" and a light. We tried
it, and decided it was as dangerous as playing Russian roulette,
and tossed the pot, map, and light method in the back. We'd
drive the RAC as we saw it.

A good driver can drive a car blind on a special stage. Over the
years you can develop a sixth sense on which way the road is
going to go. Earlier that year, Michael and I were battling with
Tony Teesdale's MG Metro 6R4 in the Wellington round of the
national rally championship. We were second overall, and going
down a long straight towards a blind crest. Instinctively, I
wanted to lift off, but Michael Eggleton, who was reading the
road by the power poles, yelled: "Keep it in, you girl!"

Michael could be nuts at times, but I took his advice, and we
went over the crest flat out. The road turned right. We had a
huge moment. It took what felt like ages to gather up the car
again. When I was finally back in control, I turned to Michael
and said, "You fuckin' bastard."

"What are you talking about," he replied. "We made it, didn't we?"

Rodger was absolutely fabulous in the car, and never hung me out to dry. The stages of the RAC proved to be both rough and fast. We were seeded 11th for the rally start because of the Rally of New Zealand result, and made a good start on the first day before hitting snow-covered stages in Wales. That it was the first time I'd driven in snow gave a good angle for the TV coverage of the event. The BBC gave us plenty of screen time because we were doing the business in conditions that we'd never encountered before.

With the snow covering the stages of the first night, we could see where the cars in front of us had been braking, and could anticipate what the course would do. I was driving in their wheel tracks, and turned to Rodger and said, "This snow stuff isn't so bad."

I spoke too soon. We got out of the wheel tracks, and the car was all over the road. It took half a kilometre of road to settle it down again. But we didn't disgrace ourselves. One of the Poms on the team had privately bet that we'd trash the car on the snow, and got quite a surprise when we emerged from the Welsh forests with a straight car.

Next morning, the snow had melted, making navigation more of a challenge as we tried to improve our position. We got run off the road in a touring section when a spectator's car cut us off, and I had to jump a curb to avoid it. Some people who saw the incident said the guy was lucky that he cut off a rally competitor because no one else would have managed to get out of the way. The trip up the curb damaged the suspension, and the crew spent 20 minutes replacing the bent parts. Then we got a puncture in the Dovey Forest, and had to drive eight kilometres with the flat tyre to catch up with our tyre support. The two dramas dropped us to 15th place at the end of the second day.

On the third day I told Rodger to call any tight ones as early as he could and started a charge, determined to finish in the top 10. It was all going to plan until the "dog-box" transmission we were using jammed, locking us in third gear. The crew changed the gearbox for the normal version, and we continued the charge, ending the day in eighth place.

I was happy with that. It was a good position in a top international rally without the accuracy of pace notes. The RAC rally had lived up to its legendary reputation. It was as fast, rough, and tricky as we'd been told, and the millions of spectators lining the roads gave it a great atmosphere. But our eighth place was too good to be true. It all turned to custard on the Yorkshire moors of the final day. We came around a sharp corner, and there were pine branches all over the road. One of them flicked up and hit the castor rod on the steering, precisely at the weakest point. There was this thread on the rod, and I had told the team that cutting a thread can create a weak spot. I was assured it would hang together for the rally, but it broke right where I said it would. As we entered the next turn at 160 km/h, the car headed straight ahead towards a group of spectators struggling to get out of the way.

One of them tripped over. Fortunately, there was a boggy area that helped slow the car, and we stopped just inches from him. Just as well. I didn't feel like running anyone over at that point. I already had enough to deal with that day.

After the rally, the team had a Land Rover V8 Defender that needed someone to drive it back to Switzerland, and I volunteered. It was a long, noisy ride in the rag-top Rover, with the canvas roof flapping all the way. It gave me a chance to reflect on my life, and where I was heading. I decided that if you think small, you stay small. If I really wanted to do this thing properly, it was time to give up the "day jobs", and become a full-time rally professional.

ANOTHER PERSPECTIVE:

Peggy Bourne, Possum's biggest fan:

The Safari was always the biggest thing that happened in Kenya each year, and I thought it'd be even more fun to get involved. So I joined a team of volunteers helping keep the Subaru team fed and watered. When I first saw Possum, I turned to my girlfriend and said, "He's awfully cute".

I was 21, and quite shy at that time, so I didn't know how I was going to attract the attention of this 30-year-old rally driver from New Zealand. Then he drove into our service area early in the morning, and I heard him asking for some water. I happened to have a bottle in my hand, so I said to my girlfriend, "Here's my chance". She ran to get her camera to capture the moment on film. I'm so glad she did, because the photo shows our first meeting, and it was such a magic moment.

After the rally, at the dance, I knew I had to make the first move. The post-rally celebrations are more than that for the drivers – they're an opportunity to talk business with team managers and car company executives. I could see Possum was quite involved with discussions with important people, and didn't want to intrude. As the night went on, people began dancing, so I took a deep breath, and asked him if he danced as well as he drove.

He had another three days in Kenya, so we spent as much time together as we could. As the daughter of a missionary, I'd been brought up to respect marriage. When Possum told me about Lynne, I told him he needed to sort that out before we could pursue our feelings for each other any further.

After he went back to New Zealand, he wrote to me six times. In one of the letters he said that he thought we should cool it off, that long-distance relationships didn't make sense. There was no

THE START OF A LONG PARTNERSHIP

MY FIRST SUBARU DRIVE WAS THIS RX COUPE, SEEN COMPETING
IN A 1983 RALLYSPRINT AT COSSEYS FARM, DRURY

Photo from the Possum Bourne Family Collection

**DITCH-CLEARING
ON THE MOTU**

KEEPING THE RX ON THE
PACE OFTEN REQUIRED
DRIVING TO THE LIMIT
AND BEYOND

Photo from the Possum
Bourne Family Collection

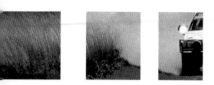

**DUST STORM
ON THE SERENGETI**

KENYA'S FAST BUMPY
STAGES WERE REAL
CAR-BREAKERS

Photo from the Possum
Bourne Family Collection

SAFARI OF LOVE

RODGER, AND PEG AND I, NAIROBI, 1989

Photo from the Possum Bourne Family Collection

MUD, MUD, GLORIOUS MUD

RAIN COULD QUICKLY TURN KENYA'S ROADS IN QUAGMIRES

Photo from the Possum Bourne Family Collection

PHEW, WE MADE IT

SHARING THE CHAMPAGNE WITH RODGER FREETH AT THE FINISH
OF THE 1989 SAFARI

Photo from the Possum Bourne Family Collection

BIRTHDAY PRESENTS DON'T COME ANY BETTER

PEG AND I ON OUR WEDDING DAY

Photo from the Possum Bourne Family Collection

PROUD MUM AND DAD

TAYLOR WINS HIS HEROIC BATTLE FOR LIFE,
'PIRELLI', OUR LABRADOR, KNOWS LIFE WON'T
BE THE SAME

Photo from the Possum Bourne Family Collection

WE ARE FAMILY

MOST OF THE WINNING CREW,
CARDONA, 2001

Photo from the Possum Bourne
Family Collection

WINNERS TOGETHER

PEG AND I CELEBRATE
OUR 2000 ASHLEY
FOREST RALLYSPRINT
VICTORY

Photo from the Possum
Bourne Family Collection

THE USUAL SUSPECTS

AT LEFT, ME WITH STIG BLOMQVIST,
ROD MILLEN, AND 'MONSTER' TAJIMA,
CARDRONA, 2001

Photo from the Possum Bourne Family Collection

**BEST RALLY
OF NEW ZEALAND**

CRAIG VINCENT AND I
DELIGHTED WITH OUR
FINISH IN 1999

Photo from the Possum
Bourne Family Collection

RUNNING LATE FOR PAPAROA STATION

LAST DRIVE IN THE RALLY OF NEW ZEALAND

Photo by Adrian Payne

FAVOURITE CAR

THE FAST BUT FRAGILE 2000-SPEC IMPREZA WRC
WAS AN AWESOME DRIVE

Photo by Adrian Payne

YOUTH AND EXPERIENCE

THE MOST SUCCESSFUL TEAM IN THE ARC (FROM
LEFT): GLENN MACNEAL, DEAN HERRIDGE, CODY
CROCKER, SOME BLOKE FROM PUKEKOHE, GREG
FOLETTA, MARK STACEY

Photo from the Possum Bourne Family Collection

HONORARY KIWI

AUSSIE CO-DRIVER MARK STACEY WITNESSED
SOME EPIC BATTLES FOR THE AUSTRALIAN
RALLY CHAMPIONSHIP

Photo from the Possum Bourne Family Collection

HOME, SWEET HOME

WITH TAYLOR, JAZLIN, PEG, SPENCER, AND PIRELLI

Photo from the Possum Bourne Family Collection

THANKS FOR THE FLOWERS

A YOUNG FAN GIVES ME A HUG

Photo by Grant Sheehan

guarantee that we'd ever see each other again, and after separating from Lynne, he said he needed a break to sort himself out. He later told me that he wanted to climb into the post box to retrieve that letter immediately after he sent it, but it was too late.

I wrote back and told him that he needed to do what he thought was best, and went back to the States to finish my degree. Then, that Christmas, I got this amazing package from him. It was full of rally posters and news clippings about how things had gone so well in New Zealand that year. The attached letter also said that he was going to Japan in February, then back to Kenya for the Safari.

As my studies were now over, I was also going to be back in Kenya in time for the Safari. "Should I let him know?" I wondered.

"No, let's make it a surprise."

APPRENTICE WORLD RALLY DRIVER 1988 – 1990

Competing in Europe for the first time made it apparent to me that I couldn't just sit on my arse and wait for things to happen. Getting the RX Turbo into the top ten on the final day of the RAC was as good a result as a European rally rookie in that car, in that era, could hope for. Powerful people had taken notice, and had come up to say Rodger and I were doing a good job. I was only in my second year of international competition, and wished I'd gotten over there a bloody sight sooner. Getting to Europe as a younger driver would have made my bid to be a factory driver more viable. Still, the comments gave me the confidence to take the next step. I had to stop working for other people, and start working for myself. I had to have the time to really get stuck into what I wanted to do.

Lucas had been good to me, and they were always helpful when it came to getting time off to compete, but it wasn't fair on the staff who had to pick up my sales round when I was away. And rallying involves so much more than just the competition. There was the car preparation, and the constant battle for sponsorship, as well. Working for myself would give me the time – not to pester people – but to establish relationships with them that might encourage them to support me.

It doesn't matter whether you're from Timbuktu or London –
there's a time in every professional sportsperson's life when
you've got to take a chance, and have the confidence in your
talents to create a career. New Zealand is a great place to have a
go at a sport like rallying. There's no class system, and the car
clubs are full of people who'll help any young driver get a start
in the sport. However, it is also a country with a small population.
There is simply not a large enough economy to get behind a
sport like mine. It's hard to be a motorsport professional in New
Zealand, because there aren't that many people who want to
invest, long term, in someone's future.

Looking back, I got involved with Subaru at precisely the right
time. We matured together – me as their driver, and the company
as a manufacturer. Back in 1988, I had no idea of the discussions
that were going on in Japan about using a high profile in rally
competition as the foundation of Subaru's marketing strategy.
There was a debate at the headquarters of Fuji about which would
give the most value – the World Rally Championship or Formula
One? In the end, Subaru decided to have a bob each way. Mr
Takaoka went to Italy to head a new organisation called Subaru

Team Europe (STE) that would work on a fledgling Formula One engine project, while Mr Kuze was made director of another new organisation called Subaru Tecnica International (STi). The latter would be responsible for Subaru's rallying efforts, and would grow to develop enhanced Subarus for the road. The decision to create their own official motorsport division demonstrated to me that Subaru were getting more serious about rallying. Mr Kuze would become my patron. Although he wasn't at the RAC, he knew enough about the sport to know that things would never go perfectly all the time. I felt he knew we were as competitive in the car as anybody. I managed to negotiate a reasonable wage with him. It wasn't a great sum by any means, but it did give me the opportunity to learn my trade, and do my apprenticeship in the sport at a world level.

Through Mr Kuze, I would be STi's hired gun for any Subaru distributor in need of a rally team in 1988. Subaru New Zealand, under new management, were keen to continue to support our efforts in the national championship after we won the national Group A title the previous year (after finishing second in every round bar the final, where we finished third). As well as another

Safari and Rally of New Zealand, there would be rounds of the new Asia-Pacific Championship in Malaysia, and in Australia for the newly formed Possum Bourne Motorsport team.

The team was a small one – Rodger Freeth, me, Snow Mooney, Chris Kitzen, and Dougie Cook, with Jim Scott handling management and logistics. Possum Bourne Motorsport started as a small business focused just on preparing and developing my rallycars. It started small, with just the hiring of Dougie. By paying him a reasonable wage instead of getting other businesses to help prepare the cars, I could keep my costs down. Snow came and joined us later as the season began to get into full swing. In the rounds of the national championship, it was obvious that being a full-timer was working for me. I attacked the stages with more speed and determination, the local media citing my international experience as the reason I'd shifted up a gear.

Taking my own team offshore for the internationals was also the way to go. We'd learned so much in the previous two Safaris and could implement a preventative maintenance programme in 1988. In '86 and '87, under Mr Takaoka's leadership, there was a reluctance to change parts before they wore out. This time, the Subaru team in the Safari would be a smaller, more locally-based outfit. Shekhar Mehta, the Kenyan Subaru importer, had appointed Surinder Thatthi to run the team for him, and Ian Duncan and I were the drivers. We knew from previous Safaris that the suspension uprights wouldn't last the entire event. The pounding they received over 4500 kilometres of the roughest special stages in the world would crack and break them. So we knew that to reach the finish in a decent time would require major surgery on the car. It was best that this occurred at a time and place of our choosing.

It was a dream run in the rally, in more ways than one. The recce was smooth and trouble-free – no goats got in our road, and the car held together all the way. Rodger and I, in our first pace note rally together, were getting on fabulously. He had a great sense of humour, and was good fun to be with both in and out of the car. In the rally, we both consulted the Halda (an accurate distance meter) on a fast straight, and looked up to see a huge jump just 20 metres ahead. We hit it at full speed, and the car just took off. Rodger, cool as ever, calmly asked, "Are we going into orbit?" After what seemed like an eternity in the air, we landed so hard my back hasn't been the same since.

Meanwhile, Ian Duncan was a Kenyan who knew the ever-changing terrain like the back of his hand. He was also a bloody good driver. In the rally, he beat me fair and square, finishing seventh, while Rodger and I finished ninth. Although the car was perfect all through the event, some people may say that I had an excuse not to be the first Subaru driver to the finish of that Safari. At one of the services, as Rodger and I walked back to get into the car again, I was absolutely blown away to find Peggy standing beside it.

"Well, hellooo Possum," she said, with the biggest smile.

It was a huge surprise to see her standing there, as I thought she was in the USA. It was the nicest thing that could happen, but taking place at the worst possible time. I didn't need any distractions from the race, and there was a little matter of a certain German woman I'd met in Kenya that year.

Rodger quickly dragged me back into the car, and we rejoined the Safari. With Peggy's sudden appearance, he knew I had some housekeeping to sort out. He offered his services.

"If you want me to, I'll take care of the German girl," he said.

Rodger could talk the pants off a nun if she took his eye. He was huge fun to be with, and his wicked sense of humour soon had people giggling their heads off. His ability to amuse had a powerful effect on women. At his earliest opportunity, he locked onto his new target, and within minutes, she was his.

I was now free to pick up with Peggy where we'd left off. Possum Bourne Motorsport was a small business in those days, and easy to run. I could afford to dally in Kenya, and spend three weeks in her company. Peggy was born in Zambia, and took pride in showing me the sights of her "homeland". We went down to Mombasa, and met her family, and went out to dinner on Mike Kirkland's floating restaurant. We enjoyed the "toys" in the Kirkland garage – including his Hobie catamaran. It was great to have time to enjoy leisure activities I'd never had time for before. One day, we were paddling surf skis on a river full of wildlife. The water was black as coal, and I was nervous about the nearby crocs and hippos. We were chatting away, when these big air bubbles came to the surface between the two skis. There was a hippo beneath us! I took off to the riverbank as fast as I could paddle. Peggy just stayed where she was, laughing at my fear. I'd soon find out that she wasn't afraid of much – including moving to a totally foreign land.

When it was time to go home, it was obvious that we didn't want to part.

"Come with me," I said, voicing the impossible. We promised to stay in touch, and I flew back to New Zealand via Britain, and the USA – where I popped in to say hello to Ken Parks on the way. I wasn't back for long. Getting prepared for the Rally of New Zealand, and the other internationals, required a two-week trip to Japan to sort through all the details with Mr Kuze. Like the year before, the Rally of New Zealand would be a round of the World Driver's championship, but not the manufacturer's championship. Once again, a lot of the big factory teams stayed at home, the exceptions being the Ralliart Mitsubishi team, fielding Kenjiro Shinozuka and Aussie David Officer, and the GM Europe outfit with the Opel Kadett of Josef Haider. Then there were the top locals – Neil Allport, Ray Wilson, and Tony Teesdale in Mazda 323 4wd turbos, and Malcolm Stewart and Brian Stokes in their ex-factory Audi Quattro and Ford Sierra

XR 4x4 rallycars. It was a strong field, yet despite the opposition, I was deemed the top seed. To celebrate, Subaru New Zealand placed full page ads in the New Zealand newspapers on the day before the start, showing our car with the slogan "One possum that won't be squashed on the roads this year".

This Possum wouldn't get squashed, but he would get stuck. Instead, it was Teesdale who nearly got squashed, rolling out of the rally lead so hard the roof of the Mazda almost caved in. Held in torrential rain, the rally was an absolute mud fight, and a real car breaker. Haider emerged as the spoiler of the hopes of a dozen New Zealand drivers to be the first to win their "home" rally. Despite not having the advantage of four-wheel-drive, he kept the car on the course, and, after Tony's roll, developed enough of a lead to knock back the pace and conserve the Kadett. We Kiwis kept crashing as we tried to reel in the Austrian, and each time we did, another Kiwi would lose time by stopping and towing the stricken car back on track. Our Subaru was hamstrung by a gearbox problem on the first stage of the final day. The car was jammed in third by the end of the stage, and I radioed Jim to get the boys ready to change it. At the edge of the Rotoehu Forest, in ankle-deep mud, they really got stuck into it. The gearbox swap, a job that took the factory mechanics over an hour in the Safari, took just 19 minutes. It was captured on video, and shown later at STi's headquarters as an example of good teamwork.

We'd started the day 14 seconds behind Haider in third place, and two seconds behind Neil Allport. The gearbox swap cost us three minutes in penalties for being late to start the next stage, but we were still in third and moved up to second when Neil rolled his Mazda while chasing down Haider. The wet, slippery conditions suited the Subaru and we were looking good to finish second in a rough and rugged international rally. With the next two stages, we took minutes off Haider. In the third, as we approached a corner, the car wouldn't select a gear. I was still trying to find drive when the car slipped wide and over a muddy bank, before slewing to a stop on top of a small pine stump. We were crushed. It would've been Subaru's first World Rally Championship win, albeit in the driver's category – as we had Haider pretty well nailed in front of our home crowd.

Neil stopped and tried to tow us out, but we were cast on the stump, although it took several attempts before we noticed it. Disappointment overwhelmed us. The big one had got away.

At such times, I always try to look to the future, and there was plenty to look forward to. Six weeks after I'd left Kenya, Peggy had turned up for a "three week holiday". Some holiday – it's now lasted 15 years, and still counting. We found we couldn't say goodbye again, and she stayed. It sure was a shock for both of our families. Peggy's sister thought some race driver had kidnapped her and dragged her to the other side of the world.

The Bourne side, who'd missed all our early days together in Kenya, were caught complete by surprise by this bold American woman who'd suddenly moved in with me.

We also had some explaining to do with the immigration authorities. It would have been simpler to get married right there and then, but we weren't quite ready for that. We both believed that getting married isn't something you do for convenience, even if the alternative is standing for hours and hours in an immigration office, trying to get a permanent residency application approved.

When it came through it was a relief, both financially and emotionally. Peggy could now find some work, and that helped her meet new people and settle into Pukekohe. We both lived off her wages, which helped free up my income to sort things out fully with Lynne.

The team's big baptism of fire came in Malaysia, for the second round of the brand-new Asia-Pacific championship. The air was a furnace, the humidity astronomical. To acclimatise, Rodger and I did the recce in our fireproof overalls, and kept the air-conditioning off. We got plenty of comment from the other teams, who wore shorts and sandals during reconnaissance. Rodger set them straight.

"Fire's just as hot in Malaysia as anywhere," he said.

The roads were as rough as guts, and it would have been better to arrive in Malaysia with the car set up for the Safari rather than the Rally of New Zealand. We knew right away that the car needed more suspension travel and more underbody protection to make it last.

Most of the rally was run at night, when it was slightly cooler, so you'd try to sleep in the day before driving all night. But it was hot as buggery, and I found it hard to sleep. Thankfully, it rained, cooling things off a little, but the roads turned into mud bogs. We were up against factory Mitsubishis, and Per Eklund in an amazing little Nissan March. We lost some time when I nicked a tree, and stove in the back of the car, but got back on to road in time to finish fourth. We were pretty happy with that, given our lack of experience with such conditions, and the "night shift" nature of the event. On the last long touring stage to the finish in Kuala Lumpur, I could hardly keep my eyes open. When we finally got there, I fell asleep on a petrol pump while Rodger took our times to the control.

The Rally of Australia was a couple of weeks later, and we put the car on a ship bound for Perth, before flying down there. Little did we know that it would take another 12 days to arrive. We had another engine and gearbox shipped out from Japan, but waited for the car to show up to change them over. We ended up with bugger-all time to prepare the car, but the boys

pulled their fingers out, and even found time to straighten out
the back end. In the rally, I drove the ring off the Subaru.

When early rally leader Alex Fiorio's factory Lancia Delta blew
an engine, Ingvar Carlsson took the lead in his Mazda 323 4wd
Turbo, while I battled with the other factory Lancia Delta of
Greg Carr for second place. On the flooded Western Australian
roads, the cars were aquaplaning all over the place as the fastest
three left the rest of the field in their wakes. On the longest
stage of the last day I drove right on the limit, smashing off the
right side mirror on a roadside gum tree, as we cut a minute out
of Carlsson's lead, and pulled another 33 seconds ahead of Carr.
At the finish, we were five minutes behind Carlsson, and one
minute 24 seconds ahead of Carr. We were very happy with
that, as both Carlsson's Mazda and Carr's Lancia were quite a
bit faster than our car. It was a result that gave us third place in
the inaugural Asia-Pacific championship, and the Japanese were
impressed. It was just a shame that New Zealand got away on
us, for if we'd finished second there, let alone first, 1988 would
have ranked as one of my most successful years.

We'd sorted the RX Turbo sedan out as best we could at that
stage, which was one of the reasons we went so well. We'd
turned the shock mounts around to get more suspension travel,
and making our own lower arms allowed us to dial more negative
camber into the front wheels, so that it turned in better. For

1989, STi sent us a new car from Japan, but it was quite a bit heavier than the one we used the year before. With the engine producing the same 200 horsepower, we lost a bit of speed. The new car weighed 1250 kg, so we tailored another RX Turbo to New Zealand's more lenient rallysprint and hillclimb regulations. We got that car down to 950 kg, and it was a weapon in those specialist events. The Ashley Forest rallysprint was a big thing at the time, with live TV coverage, and good prize money. We took the lightened car down to Canterbury, and wasted everyone with a hillclimb Subaru that the team built in just 12 days. Peggy co-drove, and it was huge fun.

She loved getting out of Pukekohe, and seeing other parts of New Zealand. She was finding the local community quite conservative, and her outspoken nature often rubbed people up the wrong way. Returning to Kenya for the 1989 Safari was a welcome break from New Zealand for her. She was back in the land where she grew up, back with her friends and family. While she was enjoying being back in Africa, Rodger and I were facing the toughest Safari for years. A recent spell of hot, fine weather had dried up all the washouts and potholes, and set them like concrete. And those potholes and washouts were bigger than ever. There had been no dry season in Kenya prior to that Safari, and parts of the course had received five years worth of rain over a nine-month period. We had to read the road like a kayaker negotiating a fierce set of rapids. The pounding on the cars and drivers was tremendous. We were thankful that the new car had a built-in cooling system for the shock absorbers. When the oil inside the shocks got so hot that the damping went away, we could spray water over them at the push of a button to cool them down again.

We had just 12 days to do the recce in 1989, but managed to get around the entire course once, and over the new stages twice. The three-car Subaru team was once again managed by Surinder Thatthi, with Kenyans Jim Heather-Hayes and Patrick Njiru enlisted as the other drivers. Our recce car was one that Patrick had used to come second in Kenya's national championship, and it was a bit the worse for wear. We had a shock absorber mount break at the worst possible time and place on the recce – at 3am in the morning, at 3300 metres of altitude, on the summit of the road crossing the Cherangani Ranges. It was so rough that Rodger predicted that all the cars entered in this Safari would be worthless and suitable for scrap metal by the end. He wasn't far wrong.

We had close tyre support from Bridgestone again, and they produced a great tyre for wet and muddy conditions. As we camped out on the second evening of the event in the Taita Hills, it began to rain. When we started the next "day" – at 1am in the morning – the road was a bog. First, there was this tricky tarmac section down the side of a mountain, then on to the mud, and up another hill. Our Bridgestones, with their knobbly block treads, relished the conditions. Traction wasn't an issue, and there was very little wheelspin. We were fastest on the tarmac, so I told Rodger to call the sharp corners early on the climb up the other mountain, and went for it. We had a fabulous run that morning, leaving the dominant Nissans, Lancias and Toyotas behind. We were hitting mudholes at 180 km/h+, and fighting our way through them at full throttle. If you lifted off, you would be gone.

Ripping through the mud, and either winning sections or coming second that morning, got us up to fifth overall. Then we had a little bit of drama that dropped us back down the field. We fought back to finish seventh overall, and first Subaru home. Mike Kirkland did an amazing job to bring his Nissan 200SX home second, two years in a row. The rear-drive Nissan must have been a real handful in those conditions, hanging the arse out every which way.

Our Rally of New Zealand was a short one in 1989, thanks to clerk of the course, Morrie Chandler. Just as we were about to finish the third stage of the rally, there was a wiring problem that fizzed the engine management computer, and shut the engine down. As the car was in a dangerous position close to the finish line, we pushed it over the line. Morrie chucked us out of the rally for pushing the car out of the stage, but there were plenty of reasons to keep us in. For some time, I hadn't agreed with the way Morrie handled such issues. He seemed to enjoy kicking people out of rallies. We'd witness a similar incident involving a local driver in the Rally of Argentina, and there was no way the organisers there were going to chuck out one of their own. Our action in pushing the car had made the course safer, as we'd stopped on the exit from a long, blind, right hand corner – but Morrie wouldn't be swayed by this argument. Mum was absolutely livid at the time. She said that if she was walking down the street and saw Morrie coming the other way, and there was a length of 4x2 timber handy, she'd pick it up and thump him with it – as Kiwi Mums do.

Subaru had captured the top spot in the Chilean market, and to celebrate the distributor Edgardo Rodriguez wanted to enter two cars in the Rally of Argentina in 1989. I had been lobbying Mr Kuze to go to Argentina as it was a gravel World Rally Championship event with similar conditions to New Zealand. Initially, we had it on our dance card for 1988, but things didn't come together until a year later. STi would supply the car, while Edgardo would take care of our day-to-day expenses. When I saw the expenses budget of $US10 for each member of the team, I said that this looked a little light.

"If you can spend more, I promise I'll give you more," was his reply.

He was right. Due to rampant inflation, the US dollar ruled in Argentina. You couldn't use credit cards, but if you had a stash of greenbacks, you could live like a king. We could go out, have a decent dinner with plenty of fine wine, and spend no more than $US10. One time we paid with a $US100 bill, and the waiter disappeared out the door. He wasn't doing a runner, but going up and down the street, trying to find enough US currency to give us the proper change. At the time, the exchange rate was 642 Argentinian dollars to one American dollar.

The boys had a great time as we prepared for the rally. The women were absolutely stunning, the living cheap, and Rodger was totally in his element. One night he kept an entire restaurant amused by taking off one of his shoes, and talking into it like it was an early mobile phone. He pretended to be directing in a helicopter to pick us up. He had the entire restaurant out of their seats, and standing at the windows to see this imaginary chopper land in the street.

There were no speed limits outside the cities in Argentina, and we could use the recce as practice. One day, we went through a crossroads, and a truck coming the other way tagged the back of the Subaru, and spun it round. It wasn't a major, and there wasn't a lot of damage, but a crowd gathered, and the police came to sort it out. The truck driver, sensing the opportunity for a quick buck or two, reckoned it was our fault, so they took us down to the station. We agreed there to pay him $US100, and were free to continue sorting out our pace notes.

Trouble was, we were doing the recce in a left-hand-drive car, but I'd be driving my right-hand-drive RX from New Zealand in the rally. With hindsight, we didn't pay enough attention to writing the notes from Rodger's point of view in the left-hand-drive recce car.

Four stages into the rally, we came around a corner that suddenly tightened up. I caught the back of the car on a bank, which flipped us around the other way, over a bank, and down a hill. The crowd were bloody amazing. There were something like a million spectators on that stage, and about 100 of them picked up the car, and chucked it back on the road. But all their efforts were for nought. The radiator was cracked in the crash, and it was a long stage. We only got a little further down the road before the engine overheated.

It was a bloody shame as everyone had put in so much effort to get us to Argentina. That night I rang Mr Kuze to tell him what had happened, and take responsibility. I hated ringing to give him such bad news, but it was best to front up and be honest about what had happened. People get sick of excuses pretty quickly.

Things could have been worse in Argentina, for I almost lost my fingers helping Chilean teammate Jose Celsi. He was doing a great job, and finished the special stages in fifth place overall. Towards the end of the last stage, a caster rod broke, and he finished that section on three wheels. We tore into fixing the Subaru so he could complete the last touring stage to the control, but there wasn't time to bleed the brakes. When Jose went to stop, the pedal went to the firewall, and he ran into the back of another car. It was a mess – the front end of the car was wrecked. I attached a rope to try and pull the stoved-in front out, but in the confusion, the Argentinian driver of the other car drove off before I was ready. I just pulled my hand out in time, and the rope caught the tops of my fingers.

The Rally of Australia would be our last in the RX Turbo. We'd squeezed in this event on the way back from Malaysia in 1988, by making the most of our support dollars from Castrol Malaysia. Our second place in '88 made Subaru Australia keen to get us back again the following year, and it was the start of a long association with the Australian distributor.

The Australian rally had grown in stature to become a full round of the World Rally Championship with points for both the drivers' and manufacturers' titles. The competition was much stiffer than the previous year, and despite the support of Subaru Australia's Peter Sturrock, we had a prick of a run.

We broke a gearbox on the first day, and changing it by the side of the road dropped us down to 30th place. We charged back through the field to finish 10th overall, but after doing so well the previous year, it was a disappointment. The RX Turbo deserved a better result in its final race.

ANOTHER PERPECTIVE:

Peggy Bourne (previously Peggy Amstutz):

When Possum said, "Come with me", at the end of the 1988 East African Safari, I didn't even know where New Zealand was.

For the next six weeks I really missed him, so I organised a three-week holiday in New Zealand. When I never came home from that one, my family was horrified.

"How do you know he isn't an axe murderer?" was one of my sister Debbie's questions.

Pukekohe was a totally different world for me, and I told Possum that I might as well be coloured purple, judging by the way people were reacting to my accent and personality. I'd hear some sections of the rally community saying, "Gosh, hasn't Lynne changed". I'd go up and point out that there was a very good reason for that – I wasn't Lynne! Possum didn't care about anyone judging our relationship, and he was always positive about our future together. However, on the way to our first rally function together, he did say ,"Don't be too eager". He was telling me to tone things down a bit, as New Zealand was a more conservative country then. It's gained a lot more confidence as a nation during the time I've lived here.

Meeting Possum's family for the first time made me nervous. Possum warned me that his father could be a bit quiet, but when we went around for dinner at Kristine's, Ray talked all night (Possum's mother was away). Afterwards, Possum said that I'd really made an impression on him. Ray was the first of the Bournes to take me under his wing.

The first six months in Pukekohe were tough, but the bottom line was that I was there for Possum, and happy to be with him. It took about the same time for all my family to accept my living with him on the other side of the world. Debbie enlisted my brother-in-law Carl to come down and check on how I was getting on. He really enjoyed the visit. Once Carl reported back that I was happy, my family soon came round.

To me, Possum will always be Possum. I remember saying, "I'll never marry a Peter", when I was 10. It came as a real shock to find out it was Possum's real name!

THE LEGACY ERA

The 1980s had been great years. They'd given me the opportunity to learn my trade at the highest level, although they'd also left their mark on me. The hard landing from high altitude in the 1988 Safari damaged my vertebrae more than I thought at first, and I should have taken more notice of the injury. The seat in the RX was a bit small, and I wasn't sitting square in it when we landed. The impact smacked the vertebrae together hard. X-rays later showed the cushioning discs between the vertebrae in my back were OK, but there were hairline fractures in several of the bones. It took years for the injury to heal fully, with the help of Victor Portelli, a chiropractor, acupuncturist, and doctor of natural medicine in Australia.

By 1990, my body was coming right, and there was a new car to put it in. I'd first heard about the new Legacy RS in the middle of 1989, when Mr Kuze invited me to visit Prodrive's headquarters in Banbury, England. It looked a much more sophisticated car than the RX Turbo, with limited slip diffs at both ends whereas the RX had open diffs. As the season progressed, the mechanical centre differential would be upgraded to a viscous unit. Not only was there a more competitive car coming in the 1990s, Subaru's relationship with Prodrive was also a good move. Over the 1990 season, they'd develop the Legacy into an absolute weapon, tweaking the engine to develop 295 horsepower, and 400 Nm of torque. At the same time, their purpose-built bodyshells would keep the overall weight down to 1100 kgs, 80 kgs less than the Toyota Celica GT-4 that Carlos Sainz drove to win the 1990 driver's title.

I first got to know the Legacy while testing for the 1990 Safari, and it was obviously a far better car than the RX. There was more of everything – more power, more speed, and more suspension travel. It was a larger car with a bigger footprint on the road, with much better brakes than the RX. Yet, despite the promise of the new Legacy, and despite pulling out all the stops with a huge team, Subaru had an utterly forgettable Safari. There were Group A cars for Prodrive's lead driver Markku Alen, and Safari regulars Mike Kirkland, Ian Duncan, Jim Heather-Hayes, and me; while Patrick Njiru drove a Group N Legacy. Of the six Subarus, only two would survive the rally – those of Heather-Hayes and Njiru. Markku's only got as far as the start of the

Taita Hills stages before the engine blew, while mine made it to the first overnight stop at the Taita Hills Lodge, but it felt like a totally different car the next day. It was all over the road, as if a shock mount had come loose, and I began to suspect that one of the mechanics had taken it out to check it that night and had damaged it. This likely scenario still annoys me today, but I couldn't really say much about it at the time because I'd made such an arse of myself on the recce.

While checking the notes, I pulled a stupid overtaking move on a bus, and crashed the recce car. It was just about the dumbest thing I've ever done – right up with the Jack Carney incident in the V8 Cortina. Given that I now had plenty of demerit points with the team, I could hardly complain that one of the mechanics hadn't owned up to damaging the car at the overnight stop. I was in enough trouble already.

So was the car. At a water splash, we hit a hidden rock, bent the sump guard, and damaged the radiator. The engine started overheating like crazy, and it took us three hours to get out of the Taita Hills. The motor soon cried its last, and we were out of the rally. Ian Duncan's car almost made it back to Nairobi that day before it too succumbed to overheating, while Mike Kirkland's car made it through to the next day before expiring with a similar problem. Of the Group A Subarus, only Jim's car kept on going, and that was mainly due to his experience at treating Safari cars with kid gloves. While conserving the car, he had to let the Galant VR4 of Kenjiro Shinozuka overtake him for fifth place in the last stage of the rally. The only bright spot for Subaru was Patrick Njiru making history with the first Group N finish in the Safari, when he reached the final control in eighth place overall.

For the Rally of New Zealand, I'd arranged with Mr Kuze to run a two-car team with Mike Kirkland. Our Safari-spec cars felt heavy and slow on the smooth gravel stages of home. The wider, longer Legacy body felt more cumbersome than the RX Turbo on tight and narrow stages such as the Motu (average speed one kilometre per minute), and there was still plenty to sort out with the engineers who had come down to New Zealand to gain insights into how to improve the car. Markku Alen wasn't having much of a run in the World Rally Championship. At the previous round in Greece, he won two stages, and had the Legacy in the top six when it failed on the final day. I felt the original mechanical centre diff was too "loose" in its transfer of torque, and the car had a ravenous appetite for gearboxes. Japan sent us three factory five-speed "dog" gearboxes for the season, and they'd need constant changing and attention.

The New Zealand round still awarded only drivers' points in 1990, and the top Europe-based teams either stayed away, or sent down selected representatives. The first "down under" round of the 1990 drivers' title chase would be a window of opportunity through which Carlos Sainz would leap to win the championship. His main rival at the head of the points table, Lancia's Juha Kankkunen, stayed home, and the Mazda 323 Turbos of Ingvar Carlsson and Rod Millen would provide the toughest opposition for the Toyota driver. Mike Kirkland's strong finishes in the Safari had him seeded fourth with co-driver Surinder Thatthi, while Rodger and I were 11th over the start ramp, the first of the home-based New Zealand teams.

While Carlos and Carlsson fought out the rally lead, Mike and I had no answer in our underdeveloped overweight cars, despite the attentions of a factory-strength support team. We didn't win a stage during the entire 43-stage rally, while Carlos won 23, Ingvar won 14, and Millen four before his Swedish-tuned Mazda engine blew. While Mike and Surinder crashed out on the second day, the best Rodger and I could do was third fastest on three of the stages, fourth in eight of them, and fifth in 13. Our charge through the 23-km tight and twisty Motu stage was blunted by the gearbox getting stuck in third gear, but the team changed it in a record 12 minutes outside the Motu school. The gearbox problem let Ross Dunkerton's Mitsubishi Galant VR-4 pass us for fourth place, but I was happy with fifth, the first New Zealand driver home. At that stage of its development, the Legacy was more a Group N car than a Group A, and a Subaru driver had some decent points on the table at last.

After the rally, I was told I could keep one of the two cars in New Zealand for the Rally of Australia. I chose Mike's as it was the faster of the two, and we stripped it right down, and put it on an intensive weight-loss programme. We took about 100 kilograms out of the car by removing the extra reinforcing of the body for the Safari, and putting in our own roll cage. It was suddenly a much more lively car, a lot better to chuck into corners, and quicker to accelerate out of them. We were a lot more competitive, but so was the opposition.

As Australia carried both drivers' and manufacturers' points, Lancia sent the full-strength factory team of Juha Kankkunen, Alessandro Fiorio, and Didier Auriol down under to stop Sainz running away with the drivers' title, and to maintain its lead in the manufacturers' race. Sainz wouldn't have to be a one-man band in this rally, as Toyota Team Europe sent Mikael Ericsson to Perth to back him up. Meanwhile, Mitsubishi sent Kenneth Eriksson and the factory VR4 into the fray to support Dunkerton's efforts in his home event, and Carlsson and Millen would start their last rally in Mazda 323 Turbos wearing the blue-and-white factory colours. I was the sole Subaru driver, seeded way down the field in 19th starting position. No one, it seemed, rated our self-developed Legacy as a chance, despite my second place in the 1988 Rally of Australia.

The second stage in the 1990 Aussie WRC round produced the carnage that decided who would fight with whom, and over what position. On the 30 km Flynne stage, Ericsson's Toyota punctured and blew a front diff, Auriol rolled his Lancia out of the event, and Millen's Mazda broke a propshaft. This left Kunkkanen and Sainz battling for the lead with Eriksson's Mitsubishi, and Ross Dunkerton and I fighting over a top five finish, and "down under" honours. Once Eriksson's Galant blew its clutch apart on stage nine, and a turbo pipe came adrift on Carlsson's Mazda during stage 12, a see-saw battle over fourth place developed between Ross and I. Stage for stage, we fought over the position as Fiorio's factory Lancia slowly reeled us in after an argument with a gum tree in the fifth stage. Although Ross appeared to be winning the battle, we were responding with enough speed to keep the pressure on him, despite encountering problems with both our front and rear differentials. The competition highlighted that I drive best when under pressure. On the fifth-to-last stage on the final day, Ross crashed the Galant so hard that his co-driver Steve McKimmie had to be airlifted to hospital with three crushed vertebrae. Kankkunen won to keep his driver's title hopes alive, ahead of Sainz and Fiorio. Rodger and I were an ecstatic fourth. We were absolutely chuffed to almost make the podium with our shoestring budget, and our home-developed car, against such strong opposition.

Our elation at coming fourth was tempered by the fact that we were now completely broke. There was hardly anything left in the kitty for a celebratory beer. We'd changed the gearbox every night of the Australian event, and when the front and rear diffs gave out, we changed them as well. We'd used just about every spare part in our inventory, and were on the bones of our arse. Jim Scott mentioned the state of our finances to Toby O'Bree, the marketing manager for Subaru Australia. Toby came right up to me, and presented his card. On the back, he had written the words "I.O.U. $20,000". It was the first, and probably the last time, anyone has done that in my life – suddenly dropped a bunch of money in our hands just because they were impressed by how we'd performed in a rally. And it couldn't have come at a better time. Suddenly we had enough funds to pay all the outstanding bills.

Toby's generosity was the start of a long-term relationship between Possum Bourne Motorsport and Subaru Australia. He would later call and invite me to come across the Tasman to meet the then general manager Trevor Amery, and public affairs manager Nick Senior, and develop a budget to compete in the Australian Rally Championship the following season. Trevor and Nick would become strong supporters of our efforts as they rose to lead Subaru Australia. These days, Trevor is the managing director of Inchcape Australia – parent company of Subaru Australia, while Nick has taken over Trevor's role as general manager.

Our performance in Australia hadn't gone unnoticed at Prodrive's headquarters in England either, and I was invited to come and help the team out at the following WRC round in San Remo, and compete in the Audi Sport round of the British championship the following weekend. According to Prodrive's Dave Richards, if I put in a good performance in the British rally, he'd give me a drive in the RAC Rally, final event of the 1990 WRC, the following month.

In San Remo, I drove a chase car in support of Markku Alen's and Francois Chatriot's drives, but we didn't have to chase them for very long. Francois retired after four stages with a broken clutch. Markku's car lasted another two stages before the gearbox packed up, which was a great pity as both showed their potential with stage wins.

Prodrive used the Audi Sport rally as practice for the RAC event a month later, and were the only WRC team to contest the British championship event. It was my first time in a left-hand-drive car in a rally, and it took a bit of getting used to. My co-driver was Ken Reeves, Prodrive's co-ordinator, and he was also getting his eye in from the passenger seat. For the first stage, he chucked the pace notes into the back of the car and just hung on as best he could. We had quite a good run going, before my lack of left-hand-drive experience caught me out. Changing sides in a car affects your line of sight, and as I lined up a narrow bridge, Ken said, "Are you sure you've got it right?"

I said, "Sure", and sure enough, we caught one of the wheel rims on the side of the bridge, and punctured a tyre. It was early in the rally, and there was still a possibility of a good finish. Then the jack broke, and the lightweight wheel brace twisted with our efforts, and a wheel change that normally takes a couple of minutes, took seven or eight. By the time we were back on the road, we were way down the field.

I tried to put it out of my mind, and drive sensibly to the end, but it was obvious that there were still issues with the car. I remember saying to Ken that the reason the team were breaking so many transmissions was that in downshifting from second to first, the gearbox occasionally selected reverse. As if on cue, Markku's transmission broke on the seventh stage. He had led the rally for the first six, and was out. I was the first person to pick up that the gearbox needed a reverse lock-out, but it was too late to rescue Subaru's hopes for a strong finish in the lead-up event to the RAC. We tried to nurse the Legacy to the finish line, and improved our position to sixth place, but I was struggling with the dog-box through shifting with a different hand. As the transmission got more fragile, it got to be hard work. These days I prefer a left-hand-drive car, as I'm now happier shifting with my right hand. I also tell anyone thinking of making a career in rallysport to get into a left-hand-drive car as soon as they can. There isn't one factory rally car in the world that is right-hand drive.

On the last stage of the event, something went "crunch" inside the gearbox in the middle of a water splash, and the Subaru ground to a halt. There was no drive – in more ways than one.

With no gearbox to get us home, we suffered the indignity of pushing the car out of the water splash. And no finish in the Audi Sport for me meant no drive in the RAC with the Prodrive team. Dave Richards put former Grand Prix star Derek Warwick in the spare car instead, which pissed me right off. I knew I could do a better job, and I'd just wasted several weeks in Europe trying to secure the drive. Little did I know, at the time, that I'd just been given my one-and-only chance of breaking into the European scene in the 1990s. I wouldn't get to contest another rally on the continent-of-power for my chosen sport until the 2003 Rally of Sweden.

At the RAC, Warwick would go on to generate plenty of pre-event publicity for Prodrive, but he only got as far up the field as 13th place before crashing the car out of the rally on the infamous "killer" Kershope stage. Still, Derek did get further than Markku, who made most of the early running in the event, before his engine expired on the 14th stage. Alen finished the 1990 World driver's championship with 10 points – all from his only finish – third place in Finland. I took some satisfaction that, although Prodrive didn't want me at the time, I finished the 1990 WRC season as the top Subaru driver on the points table.

My fifth place in New Zealand, and my fourth in Australia gave me a total of 18 points, good enough for 14th place in the championship. Markku finished 20th equal, with Ross Dunkerton, and rising Group N star Tommi Makinen.

I hadn't done a good job while testing for the 1990 Safari, and didn't get invited back in 1991. It was obvious that I'd lost some support in Africa, as well as in Japan. Not from everyone perhaps, but enough to know that we had to address this loss of support as a team if we were to keep going forward. Not going to Kenya gave me the opportunity to do something special on my 35th birthday that year. It happened to fall on a Saturday, and one night we were sitting on the couch when Peg asked what we were going to do that Easter.

"Well, we could get married," I said casually.

She eagerly accepted, and my sister Kristine helped organise it all. Peggy's family flew in from Kenya and the US, my sister Debbie came back from England, and there were members of the rally community from all over the globe. Three white Legacy RS Subarus were our wedding cars, the lead one my own bearing the personal numberplate "Poss". It was a great night of celebration and song. Peggy's family were all singers in keeping with their missionary exploits in Africa, but the highlight of the night was when she sang Kenny Roger's "Crazy for you" to me. There was hardly a dry eye in the hall.

After the wedding, we headed off for a honeymoon in a caravan, with Peggy's family also in tow. We looked around the Bay of Islands and the Bay of Plenty, two of the most scenic parts of the North Island. It was a ideal opportunity for Peg's family to really get to know me, and I was no longer "the Black Knight" in the eyes of some.

After the door to Prodrive closed, another one soon opened up in Australia. At the meeting Toby O'Bree set up with Nick Senior and Trevor Amery, I could sense that they were keen to commit to supporting a stronger assault on the Australian championship. "So why not go for broke?" I suggested. "Get a factory car, and do the thing properly."

It was the only way I could see to go forward, and Nick and Trevor were immediately interested. It was all a question of cost, and I'd already done the sums. I wrote the figure on a piece of paper, and showed it to them. They probably would have reached for the Valium jar if one was handy. The sum was $2 million.

That kind of money buys a lot of TV commercials for a car distributor, but we'd also factored into the budget of the rally team a sizeable sum for publicity. This would ensure good coverage of our efforts, and Subaru's competition in rallying would become the whole focus of the brand's image building in Australia. That was the plan. Trevor said he'd need a couple of weeks to think about it, and needed to confirm everything with

Japan. At least he didn't dismiss the idea out of hand, and I returned to New Zealand confident that things were heading in the right direction in Australia.

One way of winning back support offshore that I could see was to tick the box that hadn't been ticked yet on my CV. The New Zealand Rally Championship still eluded me. I'd won the Group A title before, but there was always a residual Group B car ahead of me, preventing me from claiming the overall crown (usually the Metro 6R4 of Tony Teesdale). Without so many overseas commitments in the 1991 season, there was time to complete this unfinished business. All we needed was the money to do it, and things weren't looking so good. Castrol Oils were a potential sponsor, but my early conversations with their marketing manager suggested he was lukewarm about doing a deal. It all came down to a lunchtime meeting in Cin Cin, a high-brow restaurant on the Auckland harbourfront. Once again, I said that if Castrol were to get behind our efforts, then it wasn't going to be of any benefit to either of us if it was a half-hearted commitment. To my surprise and relief, they signed up. We had the support we needed to do the entire championship.

Meanwhile, Trevor Amery came back to me and said he'd talked to Japan. They were just as keen as he was to put me in a factory car for the Aussie championship. We could secure a Prodrive Legacy, complete with new six-speed gearbox, for around

£65,000, and this car would run in Group A, while Rob Herridge would run a Group N Legacy in a two-car Subaru Australia-supported team. Possum Bourne Motorsport had a big growth spurt to meet this new trans-Tasman commitment. My regular guys would look after the home-grown New Zealand car, while a bunch of Aussies were hired to look after the Prodrive car. Key team members would look after specific areas of the cars. Chris Kitzen and Rodger used their computer expertise to look after the software systems, Kevin Sanderson specialised in the transmissions, and Jim Scott managed the team on a day-to-day basis.

As we'd be regular trans-Tasman commuters, Peg and I got a flat in Sydney, and lived there when the Australian championship required the most attention. We were keen to have children, but Peg had a condition by which her ovaries produced huge numbers of underdeveloped eggs, and IVF (in-vitro-fertilisation) appeared the only way to guarantee conception. So, the fertility clinic in New Zealand struck a deal with a local Sydney hospital so Peggy could continue to get her injections.

It was a pretty thrilling time for us. Life in the Sydney fast lane contrasted nicely with the quieter, country lifestyle of Pukekohe, and the relationship we'd established with Subaru Australia gave the opportunity for one team to do the business for the brand on both sides of the Tasman. As a Kiwi, I felt Australia accepted me immediately. We forget how intense the interstate rivalry is in Australia, and Aussies are often more prejudiced against someone else's state-of-origin than they are against New Zealanders. I felt respected as a sportsman, and that respect outweighed any notion that an Australian company was supporting an outside driver instead of one of their own. Besides, possums (of the furry kind) had invaded New Zealand from Australia, and it was about time one returned the favour.

The 1991 rally season started in the best possible way in New Zealand, and the worst way in Australia. We won the first two South Island rounds of the New Zealand championship by more than five minutes, and found time to nail the Ashley Forest rallysprint in the spare weekend between them. However the Prodrive Legacy put us on a steep learning curve across the Tasman, not least because it was left-hand-drive. It would take most of the year to get up to speed with the new car. We were racing a well-prepared road car, with slightly better suspension, on one side of the Tasman Sea, and a full-blown factory car right at the cutting edge on the other. The Prodrive car had hand-made suspension, a carbon clutch, the company's own six-speed dog-box, and special electronic differentials. There were proper data-logging systems with bar graphs in the cockpit so we could monitor the condition of the car throughout a rally. Once I got used to it, it was around two seconds faster per kilometre.

Engine troubles put us out of the first two Australian rounds, but they still taught us a lot about the car and how to look after it. Trevor would later tell me that were two types of people working for him – "normal" people who wouldn't get into key positions in any company managed by him, and "fix-it" people who he could tell to do a job, and have confidence that they'd be able to sort out any problems that arose. After our first two DNFs, he needed to find out which kind of person I was. He called me into his office, and asked me what I was going to do about the problems. I told him how the engines had come from Japan, and hadn't been checked before they went into the car. From now on, we'd pull them apart, make sure they were in peak condition, add any ideas of our own, and then reassemble them, and install them in the car. He felt confident we'd get on top of the problem, and I left him feeling happier about his huge investment in the team.

Respect works both ways in the rally world. As a driver you've got to have the respect of the technicians in your team, as well as those in the corporate world. You need to inspire everyone to put their balls on the line for you, and in boardrooms full of ambitious back-stabbers, few people dare to stick their necks out. Trevor was a rare example. By investing a huge sum in us, he'd definitely taken more of a risk than most Aussie car company executives would have. He needed a good result just as much as we did.

He got it at the next round in South Australia, where we wasted the rest of the field, beating Ross Dunkerton by a couple of minutes, and breaking some stage record times by over a minute. One stage was 5.46 kilometres long, and we blitzed it in one minute and 56 seconds. Nick and Trevor were standing near a jump, when their expensive Prodrive Legacy came past, flying so high that they had to look up to see it.

"That bastard's mad!" Trevor said to Nick.

I think that experience cemented the relationship right then and there. They thought, "Shit, this is pretty exciting, the pace is hot, and we're making all the running."

We put a lot of preparation into the Rally of New Zealand that year, but the Prodrive car was late arriving. If it had come earlier, we would have converted it to right-hand-drive, but there wasn't enough time. Despite the limited amount of testing, we put in some good times on the opening stages. Then the engine blew on the sixth special stage.

We repaired it, and kept the car in New Zealand for the next round of the national championship – the Manawatu Daybreaker Rally. By the time we'd completed the first four stages held in early-morning darkness, we already had a lead of two minutes and 13 seconds. This took the pressure off us, and we could back off a bit and concentrate on learning more about the car.

The more seat time I had in it, the less the left-hand-drive became an issue. To support my aspirations to get to Europe, we decided to convert the right-hand-drive Legacy to left-hook as well.

With our win in the Manawatu, we now had a substantial lead over Neil Allport going into the final round of the New Zealand championship in Tokoroa. While converting the car to left-hand-drive, we also modified the water spray system to the intercooler, giving the pump more power to increase the pressure of the spray. However the wiring couldn't handle the extra grunt. It got real hot when I drove the car on the day before the rally, and when it cooled down overnight, it fell apart. When it came time to start the car for the event, it wouldn't fire. It would take another two days of troubleshooting before we found the problem. We were gutted. It felt like the championship was going to get away on us again, just like it did in 1985. We pushed the dead Subaru over the ramp to register a start, and immediately retired from the rally. Neil had the championship in the palm of his hand. Then he rolled out of the event and all of a sudden, things weren't so bad. We were the champions! Life's like that. Sometimes it's your turn to have bad luck, and at other times luck looks after you. That's why it's always good to have a two-car team.

The 1990 Rally of Australia was just as forgettable as the New Zealand WRC round, and we retired with yet another broken transmission. We finished the Australian championship in second position to Rob's Group N car – not the ideal way round. It didn't get much better in 1992 – same niggling problems, same result in the Australian Rally Championship. I was bridesmaid to Rob Herridge's Group N car once again. Nick and Trevor had plenty of proof that they didn't need me to win the ARC, as Rob had done the business two years running in the Group N Legacy.

The brightest spot in a lacklustre 1992 season wasn't my sixth place finish in the Australian round of the World Championship, but fighting with Carlos Sainz and Ari Vatanen for the lead on the first day of the Rally of New Zealand. By now I had gotten to grips fully with the left-side orientation of the car, and knew better how to use the extra traction of its more sophisticated 4wd system. Instead of fighting for fifth like 1991, we now had enough speed to go for the win. As the only local driver with enough support to pull off an upset victory in this round of the WRC, there was plenty of responsibility riding on my shoulders as we battled through the early stages. The New Zealand fans could also sense that 1992 might just be the year that a local driver would win at home, and we were getting heaps of encouragement as we pulled off the odd stage win or two. But it wasn't to be our rally. Towards the end of the day, the engine shat itself once again, and the Legacy ground to a halt. Ari Vatanen, in another Prodrive Legacy, had a similar problem on the final day, handing the win to Sainz.

Rodger and I were bitterly disappointed that the opportunity of a podium placing in our home WRC event disappeared in a cloud of engine smoke, but our effort wasn't in vain. The matching of our pace with that of Sainz and Luis Moya hadn't gone unnoticed in certain parts of the world. In Hong Kong, the directors of PR Plus – Walter Ngah, Stephanie Kantzow, and Nicky Betts – could see I had the potential to be an Asia-Pacific rallysport figurehead for their client British-American Tobacco. In Banbury, England, Prodrive's Dave Richards and Ian Parry were keen to do business with us once again. A series of meetings led to the signing of the deal at BAT's headquarters in Staines towards the end of the year. For 1993, Rodger and I would be fully-fledged members of the Prodrive team, focusing on the Asia-Pacific championship while meeting our obligations to Subaru Australia by also contesting the Australian Rally Championship.

With full factory support, we hit the 1993 season with all wheels spinning. With nine events on our plate over a seven-month period, the season had the schedule from hell. But it was awesome to be part of a big professional team like Prodrive. I managed to get most of my guys included in the team, an enclave of Kiwi rally mercenaries, but there was a lot we could learn from the experience of Prodrive personnel such as chief engineer Dave Lapworth, team manager John Spiller, Nigel Riddle, and engineer Graham Moore. We knew we had a long way to go before we were a world-class outfit like Prodrive. People think a rally team just prepares a car, tests it, and looks after it, but there's a lot more happening behind the scenes. With our schedule, the logistics were a nightmare, and we couldn't have had better people to sort them out than our own Steve Cribb, and Prodrive's Keith "Jock" Murray.

Indonesia was a real baptism of fire for us. It was about 46°C in the mid-afternoon, the food didn't agree with us, and we were all as sick as dogs. Graham Moore still suffers from the Legionnaire's disease he caught off the showerhead in his hotel room in Medan. The conditions made the Safari look easy. We did the recce with Ari, then took off to compete in the Brisbane round of the Australian championship. It was a "blind" rally, which was just as well, because we didn't have time to recce the course, and check our pace notes.

In Queensland, we had the rally shot to pieces until three stages from the end. Then we holed the radiator cutting a corner, so we bunged a piece of wood in the breach and tried to nurse the car home. We finished in a cloud of steam, but we were still 19 seconds in front of Wayne Hoy's Nissan Pulsar GTi.

Queensland in late June is like being in New Zealand during summer, but Indonesia in early July is hotter than hell. We had trouble staying hydrated in the heat and humidity, and on the first stage we nearly passed out in our fireproof overalls and balaclavas. So we stripped down to t-shirts for the rest of the rally, tying the arms of our overalls around our waists, and that fixed the problem. We could get on with the battle that was developing between Ari, Ross Dunkerton, and I for the rally lead.

On the fourth stage, Ari's Legacy broke a toe control arm, and he lost the steering. With him out, the first half of the rally developed into a real fight between Ross and I. By the second day I was nine seconds in front when he hit a bank, and crashed out of the rally. I now had a decent lead over Kenjiro Shinozuka in the other factory Mitsubishi. All I had to do was stay in front of him, and get home but shit – it wasn't as easy as it sounds. It started raining like it can only in the tropics, raindrops the size of your fist turning the dirt surface of the roads into saturated cotton wool. The mud was wheel deep in places, and in some sections our speed dropped as low as 10 km/h. Cars were dropping out everywhere, but Shinozuka's experience in cross-country rallies like the Paris-Dakar helped him get the Mitsubishi through. It took all I could muster to stay ahead of him, but once it dried a little, I made a break, and defended it to the end.

It felt fantastic to win my first rally with the Prodrive team. It gave me instant respect, and was a great way to say "thank you" to all those people who'd stuck their necks out to get me the drive. I'm sure there were arguments behind closed doors in Banbury over whether we should have the drive or not. This was the best possible way of settling those debates, without saying a word.

Two weeks later, at the Coffs Harbour round of the ARC, we were in the lead by two minutes, when the Legacy blew a head gasket. It was my first DNF for the year, but I was still riding high on our success in Indonesia. Despite the retirement, we were still leading both the Australian championship, and the Asia-Pacific.

Back in New Zealand for the second round of the Asia-Pacific championship, and the sixth round of the WRC, the Subaru 555 team were seen as the "dark horse" cars of the event, mainly because the Legacys had proved so fragile in 1992. I was seeded 10th, and the top three seeds were Juha Kukkanen and Didier Auriol in the TTE Celicas, and Francois Delecour in the Escort Cosworth. Despite the low ranking, it would be Subaru's rally. Colin McRae turned 25 on the first day, and his first WRC round win would be his late birthday present, two days and 2000 kilometres later. But there was another blue-and-yellow Subaru to beat first, for Ari Vatanen was on the charge over the first two days. Then, when he had amassed a lead of 22 seconds, he hit a rock in the middle of the Motu, and was out of the rally. Colin won the all-important longest stage by 42 seconds from Delecour, but Ari's margin would have been more if he'd avoided the rock. At the halfway mark through the Motu, Ari was 20 seconds faster than Colin. Me? I wasn't quite on the same pace as my teammates, but helped by Rodger's new pace-noting system, I drove a steady rally to finish sixth, just behind top seed Kankkunen. I was first of the Asia-Pacific championship "full-timers" home, and, after a bit of a stoush with Neil Allport, the first New Zealander.

We had little time to celebrate, Colin and I, despite all the initial success of the Subaru 555 team. Just six days later, we were going over the start ramp in Malaysia, as the top seeds in the next round of the Asia-Pacific championship. It was even bumpier, muddier, and hotter than Indonesia, and John Coker quoted me in one of his reports as saying, "Some of the stages are the worst we've ever driven on". Only 21 cars out of the 60 entered survived to the finish line, and Colin and I nearly didn't make it as well. First Rodger and I hit a cow on the morning of the second day, then we lost five minutes when we got stuck in some mud. We charged through the night stages to reclaim the time, and going into the last stages, we were second behind Colin and co-driver Derek Ringer.

Then we hit a really slippery stage, and both Subarus speared off the road and hit trees. Ours broke a toe control arm, just like Ari's in Indonesia, and we'd identified the hand-fabricated arms as a weak point in the car. However, Colin's car was a complete mess, as he'd hit a tree a lot harder than we did. The front was all stoved in, so we attached a rope to my car, and hit reverse gear hard to pull it out. However, engine coolant was leaking everywhere. With their recent experience in Brisbane, my guys got stuck into Colin's car, and bunged a patched-up radiator into it. The thing looked like junk, but it finished, and we scored a 1-2 for the team, Colin with a stage time total of 3 minutes and 42 seconds less than mine. Despite his two wins to my 1-6-2 Asia-Pacific championship score, I still held the series lead.

Peggy and I took some time out at a Club Med on the Malaysian coast after the rally. Things were going well, and all seemed right with our world, when the phone rang. It was my sister Kristine. She told me Dad had cancer and he didn't have long to live. It really knocked the shit out of me. I couldn't understand how anything could beat him. He was so strong, so sensible.

We packed up immediately and came home as soon as we could. There was little the doctors could do, so Dad used his last "good" days travelling around New Zealand with Mum, taking her to places they'd always wanted to see. He took her to Waitangi, where my great-great-great grandfather, Captain James Clendon, was one of many who signed the 1840 treaty that ensured the Maori people retained their birthright while authorising the colonisation of New Zealand by European settlers.

While they were away, we got another one of those phone calls – the kind that you hope you never get in your life. Peg's brother, David, had been killed in a light plane crash in Florida. The engine had cut out just after take-off, and he turned around to try and glide back to the aerodrome. The plane clipped a tree, and he died chucking his body in front of the other guy in the plane, who walked away from the wreck. It was typical of David to die while saving someone else's life. He was a good bloke, and left a wife and three children behind.

So it had been a month from hell for Peg and I in the lead up to the 1993 Rally of Australia. Rodger and I took our nearest and dearest along in the hope of a little rest and recreation after the rally. Peg was there, as was Bev, Rodger's new wife, along with Stefan, his son. It was a full WRC round, as well as a round of the Asia-Pacific and Australian championships, and everyone who was anyone in international rallysport was there. Rodger and I were eighth over the start ramp, and were running in roughly the same position when we started Flynns, the third stage of the rally. It was a damp day, and the road was slippery as we took off on a crest in the middle of the stage. When the car landed, it veered to the right. Whether it was a puncture or me, who knows? The right side of the car hit a gum tree that was hard up against the side of the road. It hit it so hard that the impact tore the panels off, and opened up that side of the car like a can opener on Rodger's side. When we rolled to a stop, I asked, "Are you ok, Roj?"

"No," was all he could say.

ROJ 1953·1993

You have no idea what it's like for a driver to ask his co-driver if he's OK after a crash, then hear an answer that confirms his worst fears. My heart sank to the depths of despair. A nearby medical team arrived in less than a minute. We got Rodger out of the car, but it was clear that he was having trouble breathing. The paramedics put a tube into his airway but it still didn't look good. A helicopter arrived to take Rodger to the Royal Perth Hospital, but there wasn't enough room for me, and they sent another one to pick me up. Garry Connelly, the clerk of the course, was on board. He said he was pretty sure that Rodger would pull through, but I knew he was just saying that to comfort me.

The minutes on the chopper felt like hours. When we got to the hospital heliport, I ran straight to the room where they were trying to save Rodger. He died just as I got to the door.

I felt pretty bloody awful. Bev and Stefan arrived a few minutes later and I told them about the crash. It was the hardest thing I've ever done in my life. My mind was still having trouble comprehending what had happened. How did I walk away without a scratch from a crash that killed Roj? Why him, and

not me? The obvious answer was that the tree was on his side of the car, but it still didn't make any sense.

The news of his death spread through the rally like a bush fire. Peg, and Colin McRae's girlfriend (now his wife), Alison, quickly took on the role of helping Bev and Stefan come to terms with the tragedy. My Subaru Australia team-mate Rob Herridge immediately withdrew from the rally when he heard what had happened, and Prodrive director Dave Richards came to me and said he was prepared to pull the team out as a mark of respect. I went to Bev, and asked her what she thought they should do. She said that rallying was Rodger's passion, that he would have wanted the team to continue. I agreed. Rodger would have wanted to see what the team could do. Colin, who'd become a good friend from our time together in New Zealand and Malaysia, was a bit reluctant to keep on driving at first but I assured him that it was what Roj would have wanted him to do.

I replayed the accident many times in my head that day (and many days since). Was it my mistake that caused the crash? Did I misjudge the slippery conditions? Or did the tyre puncture on landing instead of during the crash? I'd never really know the answer, and I wasn't feeling too good about my part in Rodger's death. I was the one who rang him up and asked him if he wanted to be my co-driver. I was the one who set in motion a chain of events that led him to that fatal appointment with the third stage in Perth. These thoughts were churning through my mind when I bumped into Didier Auriol. He put his arm around me, and said, "Hey, we all know the risks."

I felt a bit better after that. When such things happen you really know who your friends are, and everyone at the rally was absolutely fantastic. Next day, I met with Nick Senior and Trevor Amery from Subaru Australia, and Chris Kitzen, Kevin Sanderson, and the boys, to go over the safety implications of the crash, and how it would affect future events. Nick was initially concerned that it was too soon to talk business, but I needed to talk things through. I told him it would be good for my healing process to suss out what had killed Rodger, and where we should go from there.

It soon became clear that it was a freak crash. The Legacy we drove that day was one that mounted the seat belt harness on the original seat belt mounts for the rear seat passengers. When the car hit the tree, it moved that part of the body-shell back, and the belts compressed Rodger's rib cage, squashing his lungs, liver, and kidneys. The seats themselves were strong enough to take the pressure, just when Rodger needed them to break to relieve the strain on his body. The doctors at the hospital said that no amount of surgery would have saved Rodger.

What made his death such a freak occurrence was that it was the last time we were to drive the car with that seat belt configuration. We'd already moved the harness mounting points to a rear roll cage cross-member in the other Legacy we drove that year, and would have moved the mounts in this one prior to the next rally. The roll cage made more sense as a location because if anything happens to the crossbar between the rear suspension strut towers, it's an absolutely horrendous impact. If the cage is starting to bend in a crash, you're in big trouble. Plus, the belts didn't come down to the mounts at such an acute angle when attached to the cage. If Rodger had been in our other car, he would have lived. It was as simple as that. The crushing of his rib cage, and his internal organs, was his only injury.

Knowing what killed Rodger couldn't bring him back, but it did provide a valuable lesson in seat harness design that prevented such a death ever happening again in the rally world. But it arrived at such a cost. The man was gone, and our world was a much poorer place with his passing.

It would have given Rodger some satisfaction that his death helped further the design of rally cars. He was always trying to push out the technical envelope, beavering away in his garage of his self-built house in Ellerslie, Auckland – the place he called "the race lab." His lasting legacy to rallying is the pace note system he devised, where he assigned a number to the corner according to how much the wheel had to be turned. By the 1993 Rally of New Zealand, 20 of the co-drivers entered were using his system. These days, its use is almost universal.

He was born in Picton, at the top of the South Island, in 1953. His family moved to Auckland, and, with his bright inquisitive mind, he made dux of Papakura High School. He also had an adventurous streak. When he was 16, he went on a bicycle ride to Hamilton. When he got there, he decided to keep on going. A couple of days later, he reached Wellington, so he crossed Cook Strait, and kept pedalling. He ended up riding right around the South Island, occasionally ringing his parents, Vincent and Pauline, to tell them he was OK, and ask if they could send him some money. That "one-day ride" turned into a three-week odyssey, and it was typical of Rodger's live-life-to-the-full nature. If he enjoyed something, he'd always see it through to the end.

He soon preferred his two-wheelers to have engines. In 1971, he bought a 150cc Suzuki to ride to and from university. A friend had to ride it home, as he didn't know how. He taught himself to ride by reading the owner's manual. After many crashes in the back yard, he eventually "mastered the thing", and got a licence. Within a year, the bikes got bigger and Rodger got bolder. As a member of the Auckland University Motorcycle Club, he was circuit racing within a year. The university gave out "blues", awards to students who excelled in sports. Rodger was the first, and only, winner of a "blue" for motorcycle racing as he went on to win five New Zealand road-racing championship titles between 1972 and 1985. In total, he collected 14 major motorcycle racing trophies for his treasure chest. Although a brave and capable rider, he was always thinking about how he could extract more speed from his bikes. He once added front and rear wings to his Yamaha TZ750, and the officials quickly banned the added aerodynamic aids. To Rodger, that was the ultimate. He was so proud to have thought of something so advantageous that they had to instantly ban it.

In motorcycle racing, his name became linked with the mighty MacIntosh-Suzuki – a racing hybrid created out of the stubby lightweight frame built by Ken MacIntosh in Auckland, and powerful Suzuki 1100cc and 1000cc fours tuned to 150 bhp by Allan Franklin. With this bike, Rodger dominated the New Zealand "Formula One" championship – the premier class in New Zealand at the time. He also used it to twice win the prestigious Arai 500 km endurance race at Bathurst in 1982 and 1985 against stiff competition from factory-supported Australian riders. Bathurst, a killer track for many motorcycle racers, suffered fools badly, but Rodger was definitely no fool. His victory in the 1985 event was so typical of his considered approach to his motorsport. He worked out a pace that would allow him to complete the 500km with just one stop for fuel, and stuck to it. The other teams needed at least two stops, and this handed Rodger the victory.

He graduated from Auckland with a Bachelor of Science in 1975, but continued his post-grad studies, working on a doctorate in philosophy and physics while lecturing in electronics and applied maths at the Auckland Technical Institute. He was 19 when he started at ATI, and often the youngest person in the lecture room was the teacher. In 1984, he was awarded his Ph.D, and started lecturing in astrophysics at Auckland University. The extra letters after his name also allowed him to indulge in his favourite pick-up line with women – "Hello, I'm a doctor, would you like a free examination?"

Rodger's thesis for his Ph.D concerned the design and construction of a computerised data acquisition system for astrophysics research into exploding stars. It was no coincidence that such a machine could be adapted to sort out a racecar. For Rodger was now tearing up local New Zealand racetracks on four wheels, having bought a Toyota Starlet powered by an Oldsmobile V8 from Trevor Crowe. It was a really nervous little beast with 400 bhp packed into a short rear-drive wheelbase, and Trevor said he never got it quite 100 percent right. So it was a challenge for Rodger to make it more driveable. He did it by adapting his data acquisition system to the car, and hooking up a video camera to monitor the readings. With the wide-angle video, he could see both the readings and the parts of the racetrack where they occurred, and used the replays to help him set up the chassis. It was an early form of the telemetry systems used today, years ahead of its time. Rodger tamed the beast in the Starlet, and turned it into a fine-handling car. He won the national sports-saloon car title with it, and his data acquisition system attracted plenty of interest.

I first met Rodger at a Waiuku Club rallysprint in 1976. A couple of weeks later he was navigating in a rally for Alan Carter in an Escort Mark I RS1600. The co-driving "bug" had obviously bitten deeply, and we'd run into each other frequently at rallies in the late 1970s. In 1979, Rodger achieved his highest finish in the Rally of New Zealand, helping Pentti Airikkala guide his factory Vauxhall Chevette 2300 HS to fourth place. I first really got to rate Roj as a co-driver when he teamed up with Neil Allport in 1984. The effect he had on Neil's results was dramatic. Neil was known as the wild man of New Zealand rallying until Rodger came along, with a fast aggressive driving style that either won him the stage, or booked an appointment with the scenery. The effect of Rodger's influence was immediate. At their first event together – the 1984 Cibie Lights Rally – Neil had a ten second lead over Reg Cook going into the final stage. Rodger, ever the human calculator, worked out exactly how fast Neil had to go to win the rally, and Neil followed his instructions. Neil reached the end convinced that they hadn't gone fast enough to beat Reg. To his surprise, he found they'd pulled another 15 seconds on Cook. It was Neil's first win. With Rodger in the other seat, he became a regular winner, and just as important, a regular finisher. He'd present Neil with a driving strategy according to the stages and conditions, and if anything unexpected occurred, he'd quickly adjust the game plan to keep things running smoothly.

So Rodger obviously had a few clues, even in those pre-pace note days. When Michael Eggleton was unable to co-drive for me in overseas events, I realised I needed a regular driving partner – someone prepared to put the time in, and who was at the top of their game. Rodger was the obvious pick of the bunch, and while I didn't like stealing him from Neil, it was up to Roj whether he accepted my offer to come and do the 1987 RAC Rally together. When I rang him to sound him out, he accepted immediately. He did it for the experience rather than the money. He wouldn't get paid until the following year in 1988, when his negotiated co-driving fee was a new engine for the Starlet V8.

We hit it off straight away in England. It was an exciting time for both of us, and we had a real blast. He was such fun to be with – both in the car and out of it. I don't think I ever saw him lose his temper about anything. He was always pretty casual at face value, but beneath the surface there was a fierce determination to succeed. This was exactly what I wanted in my co-driver – someone who was able to shrug off disappointments, yet apply themselves to the job with a relentless will to win. We immediately established a great working relationship, and, almost as quickly, became very good friends.

Rodger's house in Inverary Avenue became a base in Auckland for Peg and I. Whenever we went into the city, it was hard to drive past the motorway turn-off to "the race lab", and we'd usually drop in for a visit. If we went out in Auckland, we'd stay at Rodger's place instead of driving back to Pukekohe. He was trying to be a builder and finish it off. He bought it from his friend Sam, who'd begun the building. However, Rodger's heart lay more in the many projects he had on the boil in the garage. His knockabout car was an Austin Vanden Plas limousine that he'd chopped the top off, and converted into a roadster. I got him a new Subaru later, just so he had something decent. There were cars all over the garage – old ones, newer ones, and some that'd only suit a racetrack. A guy called Greg Bourne used to help him work on them. He was no relation of mine, but it was quite a coincidence.

Rodger was a genius at finding ways of fitting in rallying with lecturing. Like a lot of extremely bright people, he seemed to only need a couple of hours sleep. We'd start doing a recce for the Rally of New Zealand at 3am, so I could drop him off at the university for his lecture at ten or eleven. His applied maths students at ATI never suspected that helping devise a pace noting machine was any more than an academic exercise.

Like most co-drivers, Rodger enjoyed a party. We reckoned that he had a switch in his head that he flicked to go from "scientist" to "party animal". He'd say it was the bike racer coming out in him, and joke that Jack Daniels was his sponsor. He'd put away a couple of bottles in a night if he was having a good time, get to bed in the early hours of the morning, and be up again at six, bright-eyed and ready for action. This was quite a contrast to my own approach to rallying. I hardly drink, and never in the week before an event. I'd go to bed early to make sure I was alert for the next day, and generally hear about Rodger's exploits at breakfast. They'd always crack me up.

One time we were in Malaysia, sharing a suite in the Hilton in Kuala Lumpur. After dinner we went for a drink in the nightclub in the basement with the rally sponsors, and I made my usual early exit. About three in the morning, Rodger started banging on my door, pleading to be let in. When I opened it, he was panting from running up the stairs. Turns out the sponsors had set Rodger up with this gorgeous transvestite. They danced, then kissed, and Rodger suggested that they go somewhere where they could be more intimate. Suddenly "she" purposely reverted to her normal voice.

"Are you sure about that, Rodger?" "she" said in a deep, male voice.

He bolted for the door. Yin Fa, the guy who'd set Rodger up, said he'd never seen anyone run so fast.

Another time we were in Australia, and things were getting on top of the team. We'd had a number of engine failures, and the boys had worked real hard to sort things out. So we all went out to a classy topless restaurant. The food was great, and the girls were stunning. If you paid a little extra, they took off everything except a little bracelet around their waist. There was a striptease floor show, and one of the strippers came over to our table, squirted some whipped cream on one of her boobs, stuck a strawberry in it, and offered it to Rodger to lick it off. He started his tongue on the other boob before working his way across. It nearly bought the house down. Jim Scott was there, and one of the girls kissed him on his bald scalp, leaving a lipstick trace of her lips. When Jim got back to the motel, his wife pointed to it, and demanded to know "what the hell is that?"

"That, my dear, is exactly what it looks like," he said with such pride that it cracked us up. It was a great night for relieving the pressure on the team, and often Rodger's antics were our pressure valve. He was always playing practical jokes, and keeping us from taking things too seriously.

Rodger's serious side came to the fore in 1993. Earlier that year he married Bev, and she brought a new focus to his life. He also wanted to make history by setting a new land speed record in New Zealand. So he took a single-seat Indycar to a lonely country road on the Hauraki Plains. Canal Road is a narrow strip of tar over a bumpy plain of peat soil, with deep ditches, lampposts, and farmhouses either side. When I saw where Rodger had decided to set the record, I wondered whether he was still going to be alive at the end of the day. He did three runs, achieving an average speed of 194 miles per hour. It was a new record, but it wasn't pretty. Despite the downforce of the Indycar body, the single-seater was all over the road, getting airborne over the bumpy surface, and blown sideways by strong wind gusts. Years later,

Owen Evans, the bloke who helped me get into the RX-3, crashed his Porsche violently trying to better Rodger's mark.

Memories of Rodger flowed at a special service held for him in Perth after the Rally of Australia. All the drivers attended, for his sense of humour and his scientific approach to co-driving had left their mark on them all. Then we brought his body home.

The funeral was huge, and was held in the Auckland Town Hall. Drag racer Garth Hogan, Sam Champion, race promoter Brian Lawrence, and Rodger's long-time sponsors Murray Walbran and John Free, got together to organise the service, and take the pressure off Bev. Rodger's four "uniforms" decorated the hall. There were his motorcycle leathers, his graduation gown and cap, his circuit racing overalls, and his rally gear – illustrating the many facets of his life. Rodger crowded four lives into his 40 years with us. It was great to see such a huge turnout, but it was a pretty tough day for me. It's not easy to say good-bye to a close friend who had been sitting beside you in a car, and got killed.

The shock lasted for some time, and made me re-look at things, and decide where I stood with my rallying. Rodger had put such a lot of effort into his co-driving career that I felt I owed it to him to keep on going, to see how far I could go in the sport. It wasn't the only reason to keep going, but I felt that if I didn't, then Rodger's commitment to helping my efforts had been a waste of his time. I wanted to dedicate the rest of my career to him, to take it as far as it could go, because as far I was concerned, he would still be co-driving with me in spirit. I still ask Rodger for inspiration when the chips are down – quiet, almost silent, pleas for help when I'm about to start the next stage.

"What do you reckon Roj, can we still win this rally?" or "I really need your help here, Roj."

That's why my cars have carried his name on the numberplate from 1993 on. It's not like I'm looking back to that fateful September day in 1993. It's more a symbol of what currently motivates me.

Nick and Trevor weren't as keen to continue, and pulled the Subaru Australia team out of the championship. It wasn't like a complete break for they said, "Come back when you think you can do the job properly". They also sent me to see a sports psychologist at the Australian Institute of Sport, a really neat guy called Doctor Bond. I spent the whole day with him, and we talked it all through. At the end of the day, he asked me if I wanted a job at the Institute. It was good to have his confirmation that I had things under control, and could still get on with the rest of the season.

Japan wanted me to take a month off to fully get over losing Rodger. This meant there was no time to do the recce for the Hong Kong-Beijing rally – the crucial round of the Asia-Pacific championship for our sponsor BAT. Instead, Tony Sircombe, Rodger's replacement, used Ari's notes for the event. Tony, a

Kiwi based in the US, and a gun co-driver for hire, was a man capable of filling some rather large shoes. Although it felt odd at first, getting into the car with Tony instead of Rodger, the support and understanding he brought with him was awesome. It was a bloody hard job to do, and Tony will have my respect and friendship for life for the manner in which he did it.

Dave Richards also showed plenty of understanding about the things that I might be going through. He came to give us a bit of a pep talk, and outlined his priorities as Prodrive director. The first was to finish as a team, the next was for myself to get the car to the finish so I'd still be in a position to win the Asia-Pacific title. However Dave also stressed that I had myself to think about as well. If I got halfway through the first stage and I felt that rallying was something I didn't want to do any more, he urged me to slow down, get out of the stage, park the car, and simply walk away.

"It's your call," he said.

Given the huge amount of money and effort that had gone into getting Tony and I to China, I have a lot of respect for his concern about my personal health and welfare. In saying what he said, he was putting his nuts on the line.

I didn't need to play the "Get-out-of-the-Rally-free" card. Instead, it felt bloody good to be driving again, and I loved the event. Some of the parts of China we drove through were spectacular

– there were places that rivalled the Grand Canyon, and some amazing river gorges. The people were so enthusiastic as well, the rally making a high-speed contrast in a country where the ox-cart still ruled the road. We gelled again as a team, and Ari finished first, Colin second, and me third in a spectacular Subaru 555 1-2-3 that had the sponsors in raptures.

After the celebrations finally died down, we packed everything up and flew to England. By now I'd gotten to know Colin really well, and it was great to stay at his place and meet his family. In the RAC Rally, I drove the gravel note car for Richard Burns, with Ken Reeves riding shotgun. It was the first time I met Burnsie, and he seemed a nice enough bloke. Towards the end of the rally, Ken and I helped him put on a bit of a charge. It started getting real cold, and there was sheet ice everywhere. I made a call for him to switch to snow tyres, and he won that stage by a minute. Then in the last stage, it was like driving on oil, so I told him to be conservative with his braking points, and he won that one by a minute as well. But I didn't have time to hang around and see him finish. There was a plane to Thailand to catch for the last round of the Asia-Pacific championship. So I jumped in a Peugeot 306 rental car and drove flat stick to Heathrow. It was sliding everywhere on the ice, and I made the plane with only minutes to spare.

Richard caught up with me a couple of days later, as he was to be my team-mate in Thailand. It was an opportunity to get to know him a bit better, and we tried to introduce him to the taste sensations of Asian food. However, he wasn't having any of it, and kept asking where the nearest Pizza Hut was. He reminded me of myself driving in my first Asian rally all those years ago. He was having trouble with the food, the heat, and the dusty, bumpy roads, so I made sure I helped him settle in. He expected an Asian rally to be a piece of cake after Europe, and found it a lot tougher than expected.

We got the recce done on time, but the cars, and the parts, were late arriving. They finally showed up the day before the start, so the boys had to work all night to get the cars ready. There was next to no time for testing, so we had to use our experience from other Asian rallies. Next day, Ross Dunkerton in the factory Mitsubishi was first over the start ramp. As he'd won the rally the previous year they made him the top seed. This made him first on the roads, and the rest of us had to choke on the dust of the Lancer Evolution. It was bloody hard to see where we were going, but I just kept going for it. The title was on the line, and I had to beat Ross to win it. I found I could get ahead by a minute during the daylight sections, but in the dark, I didn't see which way he went. Our lights simply couldn't penetrate the dust. On the second day, there was a stage where the road was quite wide, so I drove as hard as I could. We won that stage by a fair bit, and built a bit of a buffer between us and Ross. I was quite pleased with that, and the fact I was consistently beating

Richard. As we got to the midday rest-stop on the second day, I was hoping that I could catch whatever Ross gained on me that night on the final day of the rally.

Then our team manager John Spiller came up to me and said, "Hang on, I think we've got this one sussed." He pointed to the rally schedule, and it said that there would be a re-seed after every leg. He told me to get some rest, and went over to the officials and made sure they did the re-seed. John stayed there all night in case someone from Mitsubishi found out and tried and talk the officials out of it. As good team managers do.

Next day, Ross was absolutely livid when he found the start order had been re-arranged and that he had to start after me. He was so angry he refused to start, so the officials let Burnsie go ahead of him as well. We drove away, leaving him in our dust, and I won the rally by a couple of minutes from Richard. Towards the end there was a tarmac stage where you came around a corner and on to a bridge covered in water. Tony and I hit so hard we aquaplaned all the way across it, sending a wall of water over the crowd. I was the Asia-Pacific champion, and it felt fantastic! Rodger helped – I felt he was there as we stood on the victory podium. He's always there when I race, even today, 10 years later.

It was my first FIA championship, and the first time I had to go to the official FIA ceremony in Paris to collect my championship medal. Peg and I flew in, and checked into our hotel just off the Boulevard de la Concorde. It was an absolute dump. I rang Kristine to complain about where she had put us. "But it costs 400 quid a night," she said.

I told her I wouldn't pay more than 20. It was a hole. However, the FIA ceremony was in a completely different class, and I rubbed shoulders with Formula One champions, and the best drivers in the world. Juha was there to receive his WRC driver's crown. After the ceremony, Peg and I wandered the streets, then hopped aboard a open tourist boat to see the sights of the city from the River Seine. However, I didn't see much as I immediately fell asleep in my seat, much to Peg's chagrin. "How romantic," she'd later tell all our friends. But I had an excuse.

It had been a hell of a year.

ANOTHER PERSPECTIVE:

Peggy Bourne:

Rodger was the first male friend I had in New Zealand, and he really helped me settle in. Whenever I found Pukekohe too conservative, some time in Rodger's company always cheered me up again. He looked after me like a brother when I first started attending the infertility clinic in Takapuna to try and conceive a child. Doctor Barry Lowe was absolutely awesome at the clinic, but one of the early treatments made my ovaries swell

up like grapefruit, and I gained five kilograms of fluid on my stomach. Possum was away at the time, and I felt, and looked, terrible. So I rang Rodger who came and took me to hospital, and looked after me. By the time Possum got back the crisis was over. He arrived just in time to take me home.

The six months between Rodger's and [Possum's Dad] Ray's deaths were the hardest time for me. I felt like I had to be strong both times – to be a rock for Bev with Rodger, and for Possum with Ray. There wasn't an opportunity for me to mourn either of their deaths properly, yet they were the two Kiwi blokes who took me under their wing, and made me feel like this place was my home. At Rodger's wake, John Spiller asked me what IVF was like. I said, "Compared to this [Rodger's death], it's nothing." The comment helped me put everything in perspective.

Possum needed me more than ever after Rodger was killed. Continuing with IVF only added extra tragedy to our lives with each miscarriage, and we already had more grief than we could handle. So we decided to take a break from further IVF treatments. Our time in Paris at the FIA ceremony was a welcome break in a hectic time, and we both needed it to get our emotional batteries recharged.

IMPREZAS AND IVF

The winds of change blew through the Subaru 555 team for the 1994 season. Ari Vatanen was out, and Carlos Sainz was in. The Spanish driver would go on to win the WRC driver's title that year, helped by Colin McRae's run of shocking luck in the first five rounds of the championship. Beyond these two front-row Subaru drivers there was Richard Burns – the young rising star, and me – the colonial driver with the colonial job of winning another Asia-Pacific title for the team. I had hoped that the success in Asia the previous year might lead to a drive or two in Europe, but it was obvious that Richard was being groomed to be a future world champion, and if there was a spare car in any European WRC round, he'd most likely get the drive.

The change in driver line-up was minor compared with the change in hardware. Halfway through 1993, Subaru added a new small-medium car to its model range. The new Impreza was a lot more than just another VW Golf/Toyota Corolla competitor. The turbocharged Impreza WRX was a 4wd sports variant that provided Subaru customers with a direct link to the rally world. The top car magazine in the United Kingdom, *Car*, would later hail it as the "car that ate the 1990s", and it attracted a more dubious reputation in Australia as the getaway vehicle of choice with bank robbers for its ability to leave pursuing police cars behind. With such a starting point for a rallycar, Subaru was about to enter its most successful period in the sport. Not that Prodrive's version bore much relation to the WRX in the showroom other than the body panels. Underneath the skin it was a totally different animal.

Ari and Colin had already raced the car in rallies during the latter half of the 1993 season, so a special test session was arranged for Carlos, Richard, and me to get us up to speed. It took place at Château Le Store, a huge vineyard in the French Pyrenees. There were 180 kilometres of gravel roads around the vineyard, and they were reasonably rough, and very hard on tyres. It was my first time driving on Pirelli tyres. There were lateral G-force sensors mounted inside the Imprezas to determine how much grip we had and I was amazed when one set of tyres produced a lateral-G reading of over 1.0g on the gravel surface. However, the compound was so soft and sticky, the tyres only lasted 12 kilometres!

The Impreza was smaller and more nervous than the Legacy I was used to, and it took a while to find out just how much more aggressive I could be with its shorter wheelbase and more agile steering. We experimented with different suspension arms and other parts to try and set it up for Asian rally conditions. Carlos and Luis Moya were really lucky when a lightweight arm they were trying broke on them as they were going around a cliff. Fortunately for them, it broke on the side that spun them into the bank, instead of over a 300 metre sheer drop. Tony Sircombe and I were also lucky. While getting to know the Impreza's handling, I got it up so high on the two right wheels, there were dents knocked into the lower edges of Tony's door as that side of the car scraped along the ground. Fortunately, I got it back down onto four wheels again, much to our relief. A crash while testing would have been absolutely the worse way to start the new season.

I didn't need any extra grief from the team management at the start of 1994, as there was already enough at home. When I got back from France, Dad was obviously on his last legs. The cancer first took root in his gullet, and spread from there. It broke my heart to see him so incapacitated that he could no longer enjoy life. When he died a few weeks later, the loss was lessened by feelings of relief that he no longer had to endure further pain. It still took a lot of time to come to terms with his death. Like so many sons who lose their fathers, I felt strangely, and suddenly, alone.

In the void left by Dad's and Rodger's deaths within six months of each other, rallying became even more of a focus for Peg and I. Giving the IVF treatments a break meant she could travel with me more. We'd been through a tough patch together, with four unsuccessful IVF attempts to conceive a child. She had a condition called polycystic ovarian disease, and it caused her to produce large numbers of under-developed eggs. We tried several treatments and drugs to try and conceive naturally, including the one that almost killed her while I was away. IVF soon became the only option for us if we wanted to have children. It was a painful process both physically and emotionally. When they stimulated Peg's ovaries, she'd produce around 38 eggs instead of the usual eight to 18. The collection procedure is painful, and the doctors use a light anaesthetic. By the time they collected all of Peg's 38 eggs, she'd be in absolute agony. Then they'd select the three best eggs, fertilise them with my sperm, and insert them back in Peggy's womb. I'd make jokes about how "maybe we should use superglue this time to make them stick", and offer suggestions about how it might help "if Peg hangs from her heels from the ceiling" at this time. I was trying to cheer her up. Peg found the whole process of the insertions surreal. She'd be lying there, feet in stirrups, gritting her teeth while the doctor implanted these fertilised embryos inside her, and he'd turn to me to ask about my latest rally.

195

The embryos wouldn't stay put for long, Peg would miscarry, and we'd be back to the beginning of the cycle again. Each miscarriage was like a little death in the family for her, but she was determined to succeed, and we'd start the process again.

The ovulation stimulation injections sent her hormones into hyper-drive. I wouldn't know whether I was coming home to Peggy or "Attila the Hun". Sometimes she'd start bawling her eyes out for no particular reason. I tried everything from being understanding to yelling back to try and get her to snap out of it. Giving IVF a rest for four months was the best decision we could make at the time.

In the last decade, there's been a bit of a pattern to my life. When things are going well in my personal life, my rallying seems to be going down the gurgler, and when things are going well with my career, my home life is full of challenges. I always try to see the positive side to any setback on either front. It was something Dad taught me. In 1994, my rallying was upbeat and happening, while it wasn't the brightest at home during a seven month break between rallies. We needed to get away and start having fun together again.

The Asia-Pacific Championship didn't start until June, but in May we attended the annual awards ceremony of Motorsport New Zealand. I won the Founder's Trophy for the second time (the first was in 1992). It is given to the driver who produces the best results, and generates the most goodwill for the sport of rallying. Becoming New Zealand's first FIA rally champion sealed the award for me. Greg Murphy, now a top V8 Supercar driver, won the Jim Clark trophy for circuit racers.

The rally season kicked off in Indonesia, where I was deemed the top seed after winning there the previous year. Not that it would help me much, for Tony and I needed to write a new set of pace notes to replace those Rodger wrote for the previous year. Although the rally was based in Medan, a lot of stages were different to those used in 1993. So we did the full 10-day recce prior to the event as we were up against stiffer competition than in 1993. Mitsubishi entered Kenneth Eriksson and Kenjiro Shinozuka in factory Evolution II Lancers, and Ari Vatanen had plenty to prove to Prodrive in a works Ford Escort-Cosworth. Richard Burns drove the other Subaru 555 Impreza entered.

It had been some time since I last drove the Impreza in France, and I was determined to make up for lost time. Tony and I led the rally for the first two days, but on the third we landed heavily after a jump and damaged the sump, exhaust system, and suspension when the car bottomed out. It took the rest of the day for the crew to get the Impreza back into good condition, and this handed the lead to Eriksson. They'd change a bit here and a bit there at each scheduled service, but could only do so much within the time allowed. With Richard Burns already out of the rally, John Spiller made the call for me to ease up the pressure on Kenneth, and get the car home in second place. We finished two minutes and ten seconds behind Eriksson, with Shinozuka a further 11 minutes behind in third.

Kenneth laid down the gauntlet in Indonesia, and his win there made him the man to beat for the 1994 Asia-Pacific title. Prodrive also knew that it wasn't going to be easy to repeat the success of 1993, and for the next round in New Zealand, they upgraded my car with a new "active" centre diff that the WRC Subarus of Sainz and McRae had been using since the start of the season. However, the diff didn't stay in the car for the rally. When some parts didn't show up in time, the active diffs of our Impreza and Richard's were changed back to ordinary, mechanical diffs. As the WRC drivers, the cars allocated to Carlos and Colin had priority on the tricky bits.

On the Tuesday night before the rally, a charity dinner and auction was held to raise funds for the Freeth family trust in honour of Rodger. At his funeral, a core group of his friends decided to set up the trust so Bev, three-year-old Stefan, and Hayden – Rodger's older son from a previous relationship – would enjoy some measure of financial security. The auction took a bit of organising, but it was all worth it. Most of the drivers donated bits of driving apparel and souvenirs, and we got donations like a two-ticket, all-expenses-met, trip to the RAC Rally as guests of the Prodrive team. The highlight of the night was when Carlos and his co-driver Luis Moya started bidding against each other for a magnum of Moët et Chandon champagne. Carlos eventually won the battle with a bid of $2600. Then he and Luis decided to autograph it, and send it back into the auction. They then started bidding against each other again, and another $5600 went into the trust fund. All up, the event raised $50,000, including a $13,000 winning bid for the trip to the RAC.

With the Rally of New Zealand being a round of both championships, a huge blue-and-yellow army arrived to look after the four Subarus and their drivers. We certainly didn't lack for equipment. In addition to the four rally cars, we had five reconnaissance vehicles, eight service vans, two mobile workshops, and two helicopters. Pirelli took care of our tyre needs by shipping in 1500 specially developed tyres. With such a lot of commitment, Dave Richards needed a result. But it wasn't looking too flash after the first day of the three-day event. First the engine of Sainz's car blew on stage four. Then Tony and I crashed out in stage five when the front wheels lifted off the ground on a bump, and the mechanical centre diff turned it into a two-wheel-drive car just when I needed 4wd to bring the front around. Burnsie lasted until the next day, and stage 14, when he experienced exactly the same thing, and crashed out as well. So it was up to Colin to bring home the bacon for our team, but his luck in the previous five World Rally Championship rounds had been diabolical. Dave Richards had already made it known that Colin was on thin ice, and had publicly criticised him for his lack of results so far. Colin responded in the best possible way. He won the rally, snuffing out his losing streak. Dave had to eat a bit of humble pie, but he was happy to do it, given that there were plenty of powerful Subaru people from Japan who'd flown down to see this rally. He turned his negative criticism into a positive comment, saying it had got Colin to pull his finger out.

However, from an APRC point of view, the New Zealand round was a disappointment for Subaru. Eriksson suffered transmission troubles during the event, and if Richard Burns and I had stayed on the road, we would have been able to capitalise on Kenneth's problems. Instead, Eriksson finished fourth, and extended his lead in the championship.

After the rally, the four cars were freshened up in the Possum Bourne Motorsport workshop in Pukekohe before shipping out to the four corners of the globe. Carlos' car went to Finland for the 1000 Lakes rally, the next round of the WRC. Richard's and mine went to Malaysia for the next round of the APRC, and Colin's went to Australia, the following APRC round after Malaysia.

In the heat and dust of the Malayan peninsular, Kenneth and I had a ding-dong battle to win the round, the lead see-sawing this way and that over the three day event. If he won, his points lead would have been quite daunting, so the pressure was on to stay in touch on the points table. We could have been deciding the championship right then and there judging from the way we were driving. In the end, Tony and I won, by a narrow margin, closing the gap on the points table to seven.

In the lead-up to the Rally of Australia, we held a memorial service for Rodger at the site of the crash in the Mundaring Forest, 50 km east of Perth. Bev, Hayden, and Stefan were joined by most of the drivers entered in the rally, and they unveiled a commemorative plaque set into a large rock nearby. As the road had been little used over the past year, it was still littered with small pieces of glass and flakes of blue and yellow paint from the smash – poignant reminders of what had occurred there.

For the rally I was seeded sixth, behind world champ Juha Kankkunen, Colin McRae, Kenneth Eriksson, Richard Burns, and Ross Dunkerton in the second Mitsubishi. I couldn't see the starting position being much of a problem, except for being the last Subaru into the service parks, where I might lack for space and attention. With five cars ahead of me, I hoped they would sweep the roads clear of loose stones for me if the weather allowed. However, Ross got a puncture on the first stage and he held us up, causing us to lose a minute. So I went for it, won some stages, and finished the first day in third place, two seconds ahead of Eriksson. Next day, Kenneth must have got out of the right side of the bed, for he was five seconds quicker than me on the first stage. So I paid him back in the second, and regained my two-second lead. On the third, we recorded identical times. Then he got the better of me on the fourth, to lead by two seconds again. So we changed the suspension in the Subaru, as it was starting to go soft, and nailed the next stage. We regained third behind the battle between Juha and Colin for first, and had an eight-second lead over Kenneth going into the event's longest 45km stage near Collie. Just after the start, the front driveshaft began vibrating, and the car was all over the road. It just wanted to swap ends every time we braked for corners. Kenneth pulled a 15-second break on us over the stage, and cemented his third place in the rally. We finished a fighting fourth, putting us nine points behind Kenneth in the championship. Up front, Colin eventually got the better of Juha, despite leaving a trail of broken car parts on some of the stages.

I was determined to do well in the Hong Kong-Beijing rally. I wanted to win it for the championship, for the team, for Subaru, for the sponsors, and for myself. But most of all, I wanted to win it for Rodger. The 3800 km event would take a week to cross the Chinese hinterland, and the support crew couldn't carry all the tyres we needed to make specialised choices for individual stages as the rally stopped in a different Chinese city each night. So the gravel note car, driven by Paul Adams, had a different role than usual. Instead of checking the daily conditions to make a tyre decision, Paul would check the notes Tony Sircombe and I wrote during a once-over recce prior to the event. That way he could pick up any mistakes before they proved costly. As for tyre calls, we'd just have to rely on the decisions we made during the recce.

Although I was the top seed, everyone except Tony and John Spiller seemed to be picking a Mitsubishi victory for either Kenneth or Armin Schwarz prior to the event. Going first meant I'd have to sweep the loose gravel away for the others, so I hoped for dry weather so our dust would negate their grip advantage. Unfortunately, it didn't work out that way. In China, they sweep the roads by hand, spreading the loose stones evenly over the road, and filling in the wheel tracks on a daily basis. Driving the Impreza was like steering a jet boat on the loose surface, and in our wake we left wheel tracks that our rivals could aim for. The Mitsis soon had an advantage on me, but they didn't lead the rally. That honour went to Burnsie, who started fifth, the last of the top seeds, and had four cars to sweep the road ahead of him.

By the end of the second day, we were 26 seconds behind Richard, 11 seconds in arrears of Kenneth, and had a two-second deficit to Armin.

Then they re-seeded the starting order, putting us fourth on the road. Within two stages, we put a minute on Kenneth. We moved up the leader board in spectacular fashion, gaining a place with each of the next three stages. At the end of the day, we had a 21-second lead over Kenneth. He tried hard to get it back on the fourth day, but both he and Armin crashed trying to match our pace, leaving Richard and me to fight it out for the win. We had a real good go with each other, but I had the advantage of having him as my road sweeper. In front of 50,000 Chinese rally fans, we reached the finish in Tianamen Square 35 seconds ahead. With a huge police presence in attendence, the crowd was all polite smiles as we celebrated our win. Richard and I jumped in a police motorcycle and sidecar, and posed for the press. My face wore a beaming ear-to-ear grin. Of all the events, winning the 1994 Hong Kong-Beijing was the best. No one can ever take that win away from me, and it sealed the championship for the second year in a row. Under the points scoring system, a driver could drop their two worst results from the six rounds. After five rounds, I now had two wins, a second, and a fourth on my score card. We couldn't be beaten even if we crashed out of the final round in Thailand.

Which was just as well because that's exactly what happened. On the fourth stage of the first day, we slid wide on a fifth gear left-hand corner, smacked into a concrete telephone pole, and rolled out of the event. Kenneth won, from Richard, by 24 seconds, but it was too late for him to take the crown.

The rally season blew away the clouds hanging over Peggy and I, and after the win in Beijing, we felt ready to try IVF again. This time, there would be no "Attila the Hun" hormone stimulations to endure. We used her natural cycle, and she produced nine eggs, which were fertilised into embryos. Like the previous times, we named the embryos, but number four, the one named Taylor, looked the strongest. To our sheer delight, it took root, and began to grow into the child we know and love today. After three years of heartache and pain, Peggy was pregnant at last.

This meant she couldn't travel to the FIA award ceremony, held in Monte Carlo that year. So my sister Deb flew down from England to keep me company instead. We stayed at the Hotel Paris, which was a nice contrast to the Parisian hotel Peg and I stayed at the year before. Carlos was at the ceremony to receive his World Rally Championship driver's crown, and as he is a great mate of Prince Albert's, the pair of them showed us around the principality after the ceremony. We had a wonderful time. It was a sensational night to end a great season.

The 1995 season would prove that life is full of ups and downs. Not that we needed any further proof by then. First, Taylor showed up. He didn't look too good at first. He had mycoma on his lungs, and spent his first seven days on the planet in intensive care. But he was a real little battler, and pulled through. As soon as he was well enough to travel, the three of us went to the States for a couple of months so we could show him off to Peg's family.

With the new rally season came new rules. The new 34mm engine intake restrictor took away a lot of power from the cars, and lots of drivers, especially those with aggressive styles, had trouble adjusting to the comparative lack of wheelspin, me included. Colin moaned bitterly that the new restrictor made "anything above fourth gear an academic exercise". Worse was to come later in the year, when the Toyota Team Europe Celicas were found to be using illegal turbochargers in the Rally of Catalunya. When the FIA banned the Toyota Team Europe for a year as a consequence, it effectively encouraged Toyota to leave the series for good. The World Rally Championship would survive, but suddenly there was one less option for anyone striving to become a professional rally driver, and Toyota's sudden exit left drivers the calibre of Kankkunen, Auriol, and Schwarz, competing for seats with other teams. Did Toyota's punishment really fit the crime? Banning them for the rest of the season would have been a more prudent option.

It was a prick of a season, in more ways than one. It started pretty well at the first Asia-Pacific round in Indonesia. Tony and I were leading the rally when we landed heavily off a jump, and broke a suspension strut. It took 17 minutes to fix, so that stuffed any chance of winning the event right there and then. We went hard out from then on and won five or six stages in our charge back to fourth place. On one there was a series of jumps down a straight, and the pace notes said nothing about the last jump being bigger than the rest. We just took off for what seemed like ages. There was enough time to look at Tony in puzzlement on as to why such a take-off ramp wasn't in the notes. There was a small bridge after the jump. We flew so far we completely cleared it. The car landed square, and took it all in its stride. So I said to Tony, "I've got to see if Colin makes that one". As we couldn't get any further up the leader board, we waited for him. He made it, but only just. The car landed on one wheel, and he had to bounce it up a couple of banks to get it back under control. Colin, who Prodrive sent to four Asia-Pacific rounds that year, kept on going to win the event.

At the next round – New Zealand – Colin won again on his way to the WRC driver's title, but I had a miserable rally. The car felt flat, and we noticed that Colin's and Richard's Imprezas were a second faster down any of the straights. We never did find out what was wrong with it. We struggled to finish seventh which was something of a result, but nothing flash. Kenneth finished a couple of places ahead of us in the new factory Evolution III, and after finishing second in Indonesia, he was about to put in a strong challenge for the Asia-Pacific title.

We kicked off the Malaysian rally with a little birthday party for Colin. Peg organised a huge cake for him, and a waitress held it up for him so he could blow out the candles. Then the waitress suddenly pushed it into his face. Peg had organised that as well. He took it well, licking his lips, and exclaiming, "Hmmm, my favourite".

It was one of the few laughs we had in Malaysia. Colin and I were up against the Evo 3s of Tommi Makinen and Kenneth Eriksson, and when Colin's car holed the radiator and cooked the engine, it was up to me to uphold Subaru 555 honour. I was holding second place behind Kenneth on a road I thought I knew well. My memory told me it went flat out around a right turn, and down a short straight to a crossroads. However, when we turned the corner, the crossroads were right there. There was no straight, and I was carrying way too much speed. I tried to spin the car around but caught the edge of a culvert, and it fired us into a deep drain. We got out of the car in waist-deep water, and were out of the rally. Eriksson won the rally and, thanks to Colin's DNF, the points lead with it.

Kenneth would take maximum points in both the WRC and APRC championships in Australia, with a closely-fought 19-second victory over Colin. Tony and I lasted two stages before we crashed out in the third. We had done a lot of testing prior to the event, and had the car set up quite differently to what I'd normally use in Australia. What I didn't realise was that the car needed setting up that way because the front diff carrier had split, and it was loose. The team found it the night before the first stage and fixed it. I should have taken the car back to my usual Australian set-up, but we raced with the set-up from the tests. The car was a real handful, very tail-happy in its attitude. We got through the first stage in fourth place, and finished the second seventh fastest. Then, on the third, there was a long off-camber corner. The tail stepped out, but it wouldn't come back again like it usually does. We clipped a tree, and rolled onto the roof hard. The car was an absolute mess.

Dave Richards was livid about it. I told him, "Well I'm even more annoyed about it than you are".

The crash had cost the team precious manufacturers' championship points, as Carlos retired with a stuffed engine, and only Colin finished. Mitsubishi took 56 WRC manufacturers' points from Australia, compared with 29 for Subaru. Dave was quite upset, as if I'd done the crash on purpose. In the heat of the moment, I told him that it wasn't my job to win WRC manufacturers' points for the team. I think he made up his mind right then that I was out of the team next year.

When I arrived in Hong Kong for the rally to Beijing the following month, I felt absolutely stuffed. After the rally in Australia, I did a rally driving workshop there, then flew to the UK and Spain to do some tarmac testing, and back to Indonesia to do some testing for one of Prodrive's customers. Then it was up to Taiwan to do another rally workshop, down to New Zealand, and back to Hong Kong. I was so mixed up in terms of time zones, I didn't sleep for a week. When the rally started, I felt like a zombie.

Prior to the start the team told me to let Richard go, to stay in touch, and get the car to the finish. It was easy to let Richard go. As the top seed, I was the road sweeper again, and he started fifth on the stages. With my lack of sleep, I found it hard to concentrate, and I nearly lost the car big time on the second day. One corner was sharper than I expected. We nearly went over the edge of the road, and down a steep bank. I only just managed to hang on to it, but we got away with it.

On the second night I got a decent night's sleep at last, and the real Possum climbed into the car on the third day. By then the car was feeling tired. It had lost the ring gear for the starter motor, and we had to push-start it every time after we stopped. The motor was feeling a bit flat as well. We nursed it to Tianamen Square to finish fourth. Richard was third behind Ari Vatanen in a Mitsubishi. Kenneth won both the rally, and with it, the championship.

The championship was gone, but I still wanted to finish the year on a high note in the last rally of the year in Thailand. Things started off reasonably well, but a cow wandered out of the jungle in front of us. We tried to dodge it, and I swerved the Subaru off the road and into the grass. There was a big rock that I couldn't see in the undergrowth and the impact bent one of the front suspension arms. As there were no services scheduled, we struggled into the next town, and found a convenient lamppost. We got out the recovery snatch-strap, attached it to the pole and the suspension arm, and backed the car up, flat out, a couple of times. That straightened the arm out a bit, and got the tyre away from the mudguard. We were back in the rally, but had no chance of winning it. Mitsubishi pulled off a 1-2, with Makinen winning from Eriksson. Richard was third, Piero Liatti, having his first drive with the Prodrive team, was fourth, and Tony and I finished fifth. It wasn't the end of the season I had hoped for.

After the rally, Dave Richards told me that my services wouldn't be required the next season. Piero Liatti would take my place in the team. I felt bitterly disappointed. I had no qualms about Liatti getting the drive as he was a good driver, but as someone who had won the championship for two years out of three, I felt I still deserved a second chance after a run of bad luck. Colin had come through a bad patch to become world champion after all. But Dave had made up his mind, and no amount of lobbying from PR people and sponsors who were happy with the job I was doing, would sway him. His word was final.

Kevin Sanderson, rally technician

If you ask me to name the highlight after 17 years of working with Possum, I have to say the victory in the Hong Kong-Beijing rally that sealed Possum's second Asia-Pacific title. To stand in the Great Hall in Tiananmen Square, and hear it echo with the New Zealand national anthem was a moment none of us will forget. We felt so proud. Proud for Possum, proud to be in his team, and proud to be Kiwis.

We got to know him extremely well over the years. It got so Chris and I could tell if something was wrong with the car just from his body language. At the start of Craig's first rally with Possum (Melbourne, '96), Craig got out of the car at the first service, and said everything was going well. When Possum emerged from the other side, Chris and I instantly knew something was wrong. We just looked at each other knowingly and knew we'd have to find the problem. Possum didn't have to say a word.

That was what it was like with a bunch of guys who formed the core of the team for so long. We got to the point where we could trust each other completely, and know that everyone was doing everything they could to help the team win. Possum would often set a goal like a top 10 finish at a round of the WRC. We'd tell him we didn't come all this way not to win. At one Rally of Australia, the transmission developed a small leak, and Possum didn't know about it. We knew we had to change it at the next 20-minute service. Possum came in with his usual list of things to do – suspension, brakes etc. We did all those, and pulled out the transmission, fixed it, and chucked it back in. Possum left the service park with a minute and a half to get to the start. He even had time for a chat with Prodrive engineer Nigel Riddle on the way.

"Everything going OK, Possum?" Nigel asked.

"No worries Nigel," said Possum, "the boys just ripped out the gearbox and fixed it, and did all the things on my list as well."

Nigel couldn't believe it.

AT THE CROSSROADS

My contract with Prodrive was for four seasons, but there was a performance clause that gave them an out based on my miserable results in 1995. I wasn't like other professional rally drivers. I didn't have a manager already negotiating with other teams for the 1996 season. And I wasn't based in Europe – where I could shake hands with the decision-makers of the top teams, set up a meeting, and get some kind of deal going. Besides, I didn't really want to drive for any other manufacturer than Subaru. My relationship with the company went further than the usual "gun-for-hire" driver. By the beginning of 1996, they'd supported my efforts for 13 years, and given me a chance to go to the top of the sport. Our names were firmly linked, and I was 'the face of Subaru' down under. After the U.S., Australia and New Zealand were Subaru's most important export markets, and had become so on the back of an increasingly sporty brand image projected by their involvement in rallying. The Prodrive partnership brought a lot more success to Subaru's efforts in rallying, but the marketing strategy to use the sport to break out of the "farmer's car" mould was hatched many years earlier when Geoff Cousins told Don Thomson that Subaru New Zealand was only interested in supporting some bloke called Possum.

Now, many years later, Prodrive held the keys to all the factory Subaru rally cars. So, what could I do now that I was surplus to Prodrive's requirements? Give up? I sounded Peggy out on that option. She was horrified by the prospect.

"You'd be an absolute pain in the ass," she said.

She also told me that she wasn't with me because she thought I'd be so successful that we'd live an affluent lifestyle together. She was here, living in Pukekohe, because that's where I happened to be. She was here for me. Money, although nice for the feelings of security it gave, didn't matter to her. She'd give it all away in an instant if it made us happier together.

By then I'd saved a bit of my driving fees. We'd also bought a section in Pukekohe township and built a commercial building on it – a rental property that was our investment for the future. The driving fees were paid in pounds sterling, so it wasn't a small sum once they were converted into New Zealand dollars. We were about to spend it on buying a bigger house now that there were three of us. Instead, a factory Group A Impreza would become "our house." We sold a few assets, and with the proceeds of that and the driving fees, we bought the Prodrive car Carlos used to win the 1995 Monte Carlo rally. By then it had done another two events in my hands and was a bit second-hand. At the time, the New Zealand market was being flooded by cheap imported used cars from Japan. None of them compared with my "used import". It cost us $500,000.

A factory rally car is nothing without a championship in which to race it, and nothing without a huge investment in parts and people to keep it going. It was time to call on Nick and Trevor at Subaru Australia, and tell them I was ready to do their championship "properly". They were getting pissed off with Toyota constantly winning the Australian Rally Championship, as Neal Bates had won it for the last three seasons. So they were as keen as I was to have a crack at breaking Toyota's stranglehold on the local series. They jumped into it, boots and all.

It was easy to talk Nick and Trevor into buying all the spares we'd need for the season before it started. As we could negotiate a better deal on £80,000 worth of equipment, instead of £2,000 worth here and £3,000 there, it was the sensible thing to do. Prodrive's account manager in Banbury couldn't believe it when the order came through. He thought we were the most organised team in the world, after their outfit.

Except I didn't have a co-driver, as I couldn't afford to pay Tony Sircombe to commute from the States for each rally any more. Hamilton-based Craig Vincent, who had been with Neil Allport the year before, was without a ride in the Australian Rally

Championship. So, in the lead-up to our first event – the second round of the championship in Melbourne – I conducted a "job interview" with Craig. We found a bit of road, and he wrote the notes on it. As soon as I saw that they were notes that I could trust, he got the job.

Craig was easy to get along with, quite a quiet guy compared to someone like Rodger, and similar to Tony with his business-like attitude. Not that co-driving for me was good business at the time. The budget wasn't that flash, and while the team looked like a big-buck exercise from the outside, it ran on a shoestring. All up, a minimum of $500,000 was required to keep the car going, including $125,000 for car preparation, $150,000 for spare parts, $40,000 for transmission rebuilds, $150,000 for engine rebuilds, $50,000 for food and accommodation, and $50,000 for air fares. Our fuel bill for the season was $15,000, and thank goodness we didn't have to pay for the tyres. Our sponsor Pirelli gave us around $85,000 worth for the season. When Dave Richards caught up with us at the international rallies, he couldn't believe how we were keeping the car going with so little.

It felt good to be running my own show again, and great to be working with Nick and Trevor again. They didn't have to wait long for a result. We nailed them all in Melbourne by a couple of minutes. It was a bloody sensational way to start the season, and restored my confidence.

Being in control of my team, and getting more involved in what was happening with the car, had a positive effect on my driving. There was still pressure, but it was pressure of a different kind. Instead of constantly needing to prove my worth, there was the familiar challenge of making sure we had the resources to be competitive. With that came a heightened sense of satisfaction when we did well. We won six rounds of the 14-round Australian championship that first year, and although late starters, we could not be beaten for the championship by the time we won the 13th round at Coffs Harbour. It was the perfect result after the disappointments of 1995, even though we had our setbacks. Our car had one of the first active centre diffs developed by Ricardo in England, and the early model hydraulics were vicious on seals. They gave out frequently, and once we upgraded to a later-generation diff, the car became ultra-reliable. At the last round in Canberra, we decided to enter only at the last minute, and there wasn't enough time to freshen the car after clinching the championship at Coffs Harbour. Yet it ran through the event like a Swiss watch, and kept running while the ex-TTE Toyota Celica GT-4 of Neal Bates and the ex-factory Lancer Evolution III of Ed Ordynski had mechanical dramas. As a result, we won the rally by more than seven minutes.

Victory in the ARC delighted Subaru Australia's public affairs manager Danielle McLean, and she made a meal of it with a publicity campaign that ensured everyone in Australia knew that the national rally championship was no longer the property of Toyota Australia. She was sensational to work with, and kept organising events that generated coverage in the media about our efforts. Winning the championship in Australia for the first time was awesome, and it completed a unique record of driver's titles in the Australian, New Zealand, and Asia-Pacific rally championships, but all through 1996 I still wanted to get to Europe, and compete in the World Rally Championship. To do that, I had to do well in the international rallies held in our region. I negotiated a deal to do selected rounds of the Asia-Pacific and World championships with the Indonesian GORO team, kicking off with the third round of the Asia-Pacific Rally Championship in Malaysia in July. Hampered by security concerns, the Malaysian event was a bit of a shambles. The GORO car was a Possum Bourne Motorsport-developed right-hand-drive Impreza, and by now I'd gotten used to left-hand drive. So it took time to get my lines of sight right, and to get used to changing gear with my left hand again. On the first day I cut a corner trying to get a gear, and tipped the car on its lid. It took us five minutes to get it back on its wheels again, and the rest of the rally was a mad scramble to make up the time we lost. We were charging back into contention when FIA-appointed safety officer Garry Connelly had to cancel most of the stages scheduled for the second leg of the rally, as there weren't enough marshals to guarantee crowd safety. The third leg offered the opportunity of just two stages – not enough to improve on our fourth place at the end of the second leg. We missed knocking the factory Lancer Evolution of Kenjiro Shinozuka out of third by just five seconds. Another stage, and we would have made the podium. Kenneth Eriksson won in the Prodrive Subaru, with Richard Burns second in the other factory Mitsubishi.

The next opportunity to compete at WRC level was the Rally of New Zealand – fifth round of the world series, and fourth in the APRC. It was a real roller-coaster ride for me. First, GORO went through a funding crisis, and this scotched our original plan to use the same car we'd used in Malaysia. We had to fly in our car from Australia at the last minute, and it was touch and go on whether we'd make it to the start line. We needed to find $60,000 in a hurry to make it happen, and Subaru New Zealand, CRC, Vantage Aluminium, and the New Zealand public came to the rescue. People I hadn't seen for 10 years came forward to make a donation to the team, and their generosity made me all the more determined to drive like the wind for them.

On the first day, there were two drivers at the head of the field in the rally – Tommi Makinen, in the factory Mitsubishi... and me. We left the Prodrive Imprezas of Eriksson and Liatti behind as we fought out the first eight stages. It felt fantastic to be right up front in my home round of the WRC, in a private car, beating the drivers hired by my former employers. But it was all too good to last. On the ninth stage, the engine started cutting in and out with an electrical fault, making sliding the car unpredictable. I tried to adjust my driving style to get us through the 23-kilometre Bridal Veil stage, but on one corner the engine suddenly cut. The car ran wide, clipped a bank, and the impact ripped one of the wheels off. We were out of the rally, soon to be followed, two stages later, by Tommi. Richard Burns won his first WRC victory in the Mitsubishi, followed home by Eriksson and Liatti.

I was happy for Burnsie, as for two years I'd been his mentor during our Prodrive days together, but there wasn't much time to help him celebrate. Our half-million-dollar rally car was a total mess after the crash in Bridal Veil, and it was scheduled to compete in the Hobart round of the Aussie championship in two weeks time. Trevor Amery wasn't the kind of guy who'd accept any excuses for not showing up. Fortunately, we'd bought the shell of the Prodrive car Burnsie crashed in the 1994 Rally of New Zealand, and while it wasn't pristine, it did allow us to create a serviceable car out of the bits we had at hand. Nine days later, in the Tasmanian forests, it became a winning car as well.

For the Rally of Australia – seventh round of the WRC – we entered the team under the grandiose name of Growth International Motorsport. It was a reflection of our trans-Tasman funding, and my desire to see Possum Bourne Motorsport expand. The rally was conducted in the middle of a flood. Heavy rain forced the cancellation of two stages, and most of the others were shortened. With a strong field of WRC teams, we concentrated on scoring maximum points in the local championship as the international rally was also the 12th round of the ARC. Our job was made easier by Neal Bates suffering suspension trouble, and Ed Ordynski getting a string of punctures. Seven factory WRC cars finished in front of us, with winner Tommi Makinen wrapping up his first driver's title. We drove a steady rally through the mud and gloop to finish eighth, 17 minutes in front of our nearest ARC rival – Ordynski.

It wasn't a bad season, although a strong finish in New Zealand would have made me much happier. We did the business for Subaru Australia, and showed good potential in the international events. In Australia and Malaysia, we were the first of the private teams and could take some satisfaction in what we achieved without factory support. But it wasn't easy. We struggled to finance the 1996 campaign, and our rally-to-rally existence put a lot of pressure on everyone in the team. I was determined to ensure that our future campaigns were built on stronger financial foundations. I also wanted to give something back to the sport by supporting a younger driver in a Group N Impreza. In 1996 we ran a Group N car for Greg Graham in the New Zealand championship, and he showed a lot of promise. For the coming season, I wanted Greg to run in the Australian championship as well.

Possum Bourne Motorsport was growing under the management of Steve Cribb. The crew of Doug Cook, Ray Swain, Kevin Sanderson, Wayne Rodgers, and Richard Rowland weren't just preparing my cars anymore. There were cars prepared for customers in Australia, Japan, Indonesia and Taiwan, as well as New Zealand. Pukekohe was rapidly becoming the hub of rallycar development for the region.

Changes to the rules for 1997 ushered in the "World Rally Car" era of the FIA championships. These allowed more freedom to modify the cars. The floorpan could be cut into and strengthened, and the wheel tracks extended to lower the car's centre of gravity. The "World Rally" regs would result in an unparalleled period of performance parity between the factory cars from Subaru, Mitsubishi, Ford, and Toyota. At the 1997 San Remo rally, just 14 seconds separated the top four finishers. However, for the privateer who could only afford a veteran Group A car from previous seasons, the gap in competitiveness had just got a lot wider. There was little or no chance of beating the 'hand made' World Rally Cars with a production-based vehicle. So we pulled our horns in a little for 1997, and stuck to our knitting. We'd defend the Aussie title, and do just the two WRC rounds we had on our back doorstep – Australia and New Zealand.

When I went to Japan to discuss the coming season with STi, they held a little ceremony for me to celebrate 14 years of working together. There was obviously going to be some gift of some kind, and I expected to receive a gold watch or something similar. To my surprise they handed me a set of car keys. They belonged to the jet-black Impreza WRX STi I'd admired outside on my way into the building. It was a wonderful gesture, and it was nice to know my loyalty was highly regarded. When I got it back to New Zealand, the black STi became my "Sunday drive" car for weekends when I wasn't rallying.

In our new strategy of doing fewer rallies, but doing the ones we entered more thoroughly, we skipped the first round of the 1997 ARC in Perth, and let Neal Bates develop a lead in the shorter five-round series. With the best four results counting towards the title, we needed to do well in the final four rounds. The second round in Queensland set us up nicely to defend the title. We put a lot of late nights into preparing a new car, and it went great all through the rally. There wasn't time to fully test it though, as we finished building it on the Friday before the start. It was a great debut for the new Impreza, and with the performance of each day of the two-day event counting towards the championship, we scored the maximum amount we could. On the Saturday, we finished 13 seconds in front of Neal after a close battle. On the Sunday, his Group A Toyota Celica struck electrical problems, and did not finish. We left Queensland in third place on the points table, four behind Ed Ordynski, and 26 behind Neal.

At the next round in Coffs Harbour, Ed traded his Group N Lancer for a full Ralliart-developed Group A version, which made him suddenly a lot more competitive, and the title developed into a three-way race. The Pukekohe-prepared Impreza was equal to the new challenge however, and Craig and I put a 10-second lead on Ed and Neal in the first of the forest stages. That performance set the tone for the day. Apart from the super-special stage in the Coffs Harbour showgrounds (won by a delighted Greg Alexander), and the last stage of the day (won by two seconds by Neal after we backed off in his dust), we won every stage to win the day by one minute from Ed.

Next day, it was business as usual. We got stuck into it from the start, and in two stages, developed enough of a lead to ensure that Ed and Neal were left scrapping over second. They traded blow for blow for the rest of the rally, Neal eventually getting the better of Ed by two seconds. Our win of the second day completed another maximum points score for Subaru Australia, and the icing on the cake was Greg's win in the Group N class on both days. After his problems in Perth, and a roll in Queensland, Greg was beginning a successful bid to win the Group N title that year, and his performance put Subaru on track to take out the manufacturers' title. There were a few beers sunk by the team that Sunday night.

Toyota Australia were very keen to get "their" title back, and for the rest of the championship Neal drove a new TTE-sourced factory Corolla World Rally Car. It was two million bucks worth of high-tech Toyota. When I first saw it I knew defending the driver's title wasn't going to be easy. With his 30 points from Coffs to my 40, Neal still had the points lead, and now he had the best car Toyota could give him to defend it. However, Neal was having his first season driving on the left side of the car, and in the final countdown to the title, a bigger challenge would emerge from another state and another manufacturer. Down in Adelaide, South Australia, Ed Ordynski was finalising a deal with Mitsubishi Motors Australia to keep the Ralliart Group A car for the rest of the season. The championship would go right to the wire in the final round at Melbourne.

Competing in the Rally of New Zealand could hardly be called "time out" from the Australian championship. Neal was there (in the Group A Celica), along with six factory World Rally cars from Subaru, Mitsubishi, and Ford. It was a rally most fans will recall for the way a suicidal sheep ruined any chance Carlos Sainz had of winning it, rather than our steady drive to fifth place, and the honour of being the first non-WRC car home, first privateer, and first Kiwi. Reporters later called my drive "unusually restrained", and "spectacular but disciplined". I definitely preferred the latter description. There was a race going on within the race. Beating Neal would give me a psychological boost for the Australian championship, and vice versa. So I felt happy with fifth, five minutes in front of Neal – who finished sixth in his first event in New Zealand.

If I had the upper hand, mentally, going to Melbourne, I lost it on the first leg of the rally. We started out confidently enough, and established a slight lead. The new Corolla had definitely shut down any opportunity for us to establish a decisive lead to defend, and Neal was going for it. As was Ed in the Ralliart Evo. When we punctured a tyre on stage four, and drove the last eight kilometres on the wheel rim, I could feel the championship starting to slip away. Neal took full advantage to win the first leg by 48 seconds from Ed. We were third, but took some consolation in Greg's fine two-minute victory over Mitsubishi's Michael Guest in the Group N class.

Three drivers could win the championship going into the second leg in Melbourne, and two "moments" decided the championship in our favour. The first was when the rear driveshaft snapped in Neal's Corolla on the third stage, forcing him to complete the leg with a front-drive Toyota. That effectively left Ed and I scrapping over the title. We had a real ding-dong battle going until the penultimate stage, when Ed spun the Lancer, and handed the victory to me. I was the Australian champion for the second consecutive year with 154 points to Ed's 150, and

Neal's 131. Greg wasn't quite as lucky. He finished fourth behind Michael Guest, and lost the Group N title by a narrow margin.

When he came to New Zealand earlier in the year, Neal definitely wanted to beat me on my home soil, and I was just as keen to beat him at the Rally of Australia – especially now he had the Corolla World Rally Car to drive. Neal was inducted into Toyota Team Europe for the rally, and had the full support of the world championship technicians. He came out fighting, and finished third equal with the factory Subaru of Eriksson and the factory Lancer of Tommi Makinen at the opening super special stage of the rally at Langley Park. It was a more competitive field in Australia, with factory teams from Seat and Toyota expanding the usual suspects of Subaru, Mitsubishi and Ford in down-under WRC rounds. Craig and I started conservatively, finishing in the top 10 on the opening stages. As the rally took its toll on the cars, we moved up the order. Neal struck transmission problems, and left the road for a minute, dropping him down the leaderboard. We stuck to our pace right through the rally, the car running faultlessly. The eighth and seventh fastest stage times quickly turned into sixth and fifth fastest. We finished fifth again, first privateer, and top finisher of the Australian Rally Championship contenders. Ed brought the Ralliart Lancer home sixth, in front of the factory-supported Celica of Freddy Loix. Neal was eighth.

At the Rally of Australia that year I got the biggest surprise. It was a phone call from Peg during the recce. I knew she had been having problems with stomach pains, and we were both taking these symptoms quite seriously. She'd seen the doctor that morning back in New Zealand for further tests, and this call might've confirmed whether she had cancer. Instead, she told me she was pregnant. I nearly fell out of the recce car.

Things were shaping up well for the 1998 season until the downturn in the Asian economy kicked us in the guts. I had arranged backing with an Indonesian sponsor to do a full Asia-Pacific championship campaign, as well as the Australian Rally championship for Subaru Australia. The deal would allow us to purchase one of the WRC '97-spec Imprezas from Prodrive, and I couldn't wait to drive it. However, the bursting of the economic bubble gave the sponsor cold feet just days before we were due to sign the deal. For 1998, we'd have to make do with the support we had at hand. That meant concentrating on the Australian championship, with just the one event outside Australia – the Rally of New Zealand. We weren't the only ones affected by the economic downturn. After losing the driver's title in the ARC so narrowly in 1997, Mitsubishi Motors Australia pulled out in 1998. Ed sat on the sidelines, while Michael Guest had a one-off drive in one of our Group N cars at the Rally of Queensland, where he joined our new team-mate Cody Crocker.

Cody joined the team at the second event of the series – the Forrest Rally in Perth. He proved his worth straight away by winning the Group N class in the first leg, and finishing second in the class the following day. Up front was another blue and yellow Subaru, and it would be a familiar sight throughout the season, with Craig and I winning the first eight legs of the series. Although the final round of the championship in Melbourne now carried double the points of the others, by the time we got there we had only to finish fifth on both days to clinch our third driver's title. In Melbourne we drove to get the car home, as a DNF would have proved a lot more costly than finishing fifth. Neal won both legs in the Corolla WRC, while we bought the Group A Impreza home second on both days. It was enough to win the title by 40 points. Cody capped a fine season by winning the Group N crown, and helped the Subaru Australia team win the manufacturers' honours.

While things went well in Australia in 1998 – including the international rally where we finished eighth behind seven factory WRC cars, they didn't go so well in New Zealand. We managed to complete just three stages of our home rally before retiring in the fourth.

This made me all the more determined to do better in 1999, when I'd finally drive a World Rally Car. We bought the Prodrive car Colin McRae used in the Rally of Australia, and it was absolutely awesome compared with what we had been driving. It was a dream machine, and if you asked me what was the favourite car I ever drove, this one would be second on the list after our 2000-spec World Rally Car. The difference was phenomenal. How different? In the previous season I struggled to get into the top 10 on the opening stages of the Rally of New Zealand. One year later, in the WRC car, I came out and won the first super special at Manukau City. There was a huge crowd watching, and they just went nuts. Trevor Amery and Nick Senior were there as well, and they were really chuffed that their boy did the business against all the WRC heavyweights. It was an unforgettable evening.

With the Impreza WRC, I felt we could conduct a successful Asia-Pacific campaign as well as win the Australian Rally Championship. The Canberra round of the ARC, and the New Zealand round of the WRC both carried points for the APRC, and if I did well in them, it would be worth going to mainland Asia to finish off the Asia-Pacific championship. But it wasn't to be. Craig and I had Canberra shot to bits – Neal had retired the Corolla with a cooked engine, and we had amassed a lead of more than six minutes on Yoshio Kataoka in a Ralliart Lancer. Then I cut a corner and hit a tree stump I couldn't see in the grass. It broke the front left suspension, and we limped out of the stage. The crew tore into fixing the damage, but it was too late – our lead had evaporated. There were two stages left to catch Kataoka. We took 21 seconds off him in 10 kilometres on the first, and 72 seconds off him in the second, but it wasn't enough. We had to be content with second – a result that still kept our hopes for the Australian Rally Championship alive.

Doing well in New Zealand would have also kept our Asia-Pacific aspirations alive but the rest of the rally didn't quite live up to the promise of the opening stage. As we drove over the stages, the crowd kept egging us on, some of the fans timing the gaps between us and the cars in front, and letting us know if we were catching them or falling behind. We'd finish fifth in the end – which wasn't bad considering we beat the factory WRC Corollas of Carlos Sainz and Matthias Kahle, and Freddy Loix in the other factory Mitsubishi. I still rate the 1999 effort as my best performance in my home rally. The competition was a lot tougher than in 1987 when I finished third. However, getting the support needed to go to other Asia-Pacific rounds that year was dependent on taking the points lead in New Zealand, and we were tied for the top position on the points table with Yoshio. A third Asia-Pacific title would have to wait until the following year.

So we concentrated on the business at hand, and cleaned up the Aussie title for the fourth time in a row. Once again, the biggest challenge came from Neal, who won three heats to our five. Cody was Group N champion for the second year in a row.

Our performance in the Rally of New Zealand didn't go unnoticed. It helped us win the support of Caltex Oils, who got behind our efforts in the 2000 season. We would compete in the Asia-Pacific championship wearing their colours to promote their high-performance oil – Havoline – in Asian markets. Our WRC Impreza would stay in Australia for Craig and I to compete in the ARC, while a second Group A Impreza would move around Asia, with Mark Stacey scheduled for pace note duty during the mainland Asian rounds. Mark had plenty of experience under his belt. He'd guided Ed Ordynski to four consecutive Australian Group N championships from 1993 to 1996, as well as Barry Lowe to the 1986 Australian driver's crown in an RX Turbo. He was an Aussie, who'd worked for Mitsubishi, but I wasn't going to hold anything against him for either of those things. I have been really lucky with the people who've jumped in the passenger's seat with me. From Ken, through Michael, Rodger, Tony, and Craig, to Mark, they've always been very good, and it's a darn sight easier to drive well when you don't have to worry about what the passenger is doing.

For us, the 2000 Asia-Pacific championship kicked off at the second round in Canberra – also a round of the Australian championship. By then our main competition in the form of Malaysia's Karamjit Singh and the factory Proton PERT rally car had already established a points lead by winning the first round in Indonesia. We put our hand up for the title straight away with an emphatic victory in Canberra. After a nervous start when a puncture dropped us to 10th place on the first stage, we won 17 of the 21 stages to finish 6 minutes and 21 seconds ahead of Katsuhiko Taguchi in a Ralliart Lancer.

At the following round at the Rally of New Zealand, our charge up the APRC points table was halted slightly by Petter Solberg's fine drive in a Ford Focus WRC to fourth place in my home rally. Craig and I finished sixth overall, and second APRC contender home. It was enough to take over the points lead from Singh and Taguchi, who both came down to New Zealand to compete but went home without adding to their tally. Katsuhiko's rally lasted just 12 kilometres before he crashed out.

At the fourth round in China, Mark and I led from start to finish, winning all 13 stages. But then, Karamjit's sponsor, Malaysian Airlines, made it easier for us by shipping his rallycar, recce car, and service trucks to the USA instead of China. They flew in another car at the 11th hour for him, but it can't have done his chances much good.

Victory in China set us up to win the title at the fifth round in Karamjit's home rally in Malaysia. We arrived 21 points in the lead, but knew Karamjit would be tough to beat on roads he knew like the back of his hand. I had plenty of confidence in my driving, having just wrapped up my fifth consecutive Australian driver's championship with Craig the previous weekend. We quickly established a lead on the factory Proton, then went into cruise control on the final day. The weather was superb, the car performed brilliantly, and Stace and I were really pumped up by all the spectators who turned out in force. We basically had fun for the rest of the rally, enjoying sliding around the dusty roads, and the cheers of the crowd. When we finished, I was Asia-Pacific champion for the third time, and it felt all the more satisfying because I knew it was with my own privately-entered team. Karamjit would extract some revenge at the sixth round in Thailand, establishing a lead of three minutes going into the final day after our Subaru suffered a puncture and diff problems. We charged back at him, driving at the limit, and beyond. We sailed so high over the jumps we cracked the windscreen and buckled the roof on the landings, but it was all too late. Karamjit won the event by 36 seconds.

He won that final victory, but we won the war. As a three-time Asia-Pacific and five-time Australian champion, life was good. There was a new daughter waiting for me at home, and to cap it all off, Peggy was able to join me in Monte Carlo as I accepted my 2000 Asia-Pacific Rally Champion FIA trophy.

OTHER PERSPECTIVES:

Peggy Bourne:

Little did Possum and I know that we conceived Spencer when I returned home from a visit to the US to see my Mum. When morning sickness started to affect me, pregnancy was the last thing we thought could be causing the nausea. When I went to the doctor, she suggested we test for everything else. When those tests proved negative, she said, "OK, I'm going to have to give you a pregnancy test." I told her that it was impossible for me to be pregnant, but she insisted.

She started bawling her eyes out when she saw the result. That started me crying as well. We rang Possum in Australia straight away. He thought there must be something seriously wrong at first because of the way we were both cracking up. I was four and a half months pregnant already. The doctors said it was a million to one chance that we had Spencer.

When he was four months old, I was visiting the doctor again, and she said, "You know that cancer we talked about last year? Well, I think you've got it again."

Our daughter Jazlin was on her way.

I was so proud of Possum for winning the APRC in 2000. He put together a great package, and with a fantastic positive attitude achieved his dream of winning the title with his own dedicated team.

Mark Stacey:

Possum would have to be the best driver I ever rode shotgun for. He was just so professional and talented, and one of the few that owned and ran a team, and chased the sponsorship dollars to run that team. There's many a talented driver that could have done extremely well but they didn't have the ability to create the income to do it. Possum won the APRC a couple of times with Prodrive, and once with his own team. It is unrealistic to believe you can get into the WRC unless you can find a million-dollar sponsor that wants you to be involved, knowing that you are not going to be in a factory car and you are going to have trouble beating the factory cars.

Chris Kitzen, rally technician

Kevin and I looked after the front half of the car. From 1996 to 2003, I only missed one event – Perth at the start of the 2003 Australian Rally Championship. I sent an email to Possum, wishing him luck, and telling him he wouldn't have to look at my bald head bobbing around underneath the car. He replied, saying, "Yes, it feels pretty odd without Kev and you here. It's just not the same – grab a plane over if you want."

In 2000, I spent 103 days away from work chasing Possum around the world. I had to get an extra page added to my passport. We'd always have to carry excess baggage, and got to know the people at airports pretty well. They'd ask, "So where are you guys off to this week?" while wondering what to do with our bags full of spare parts and tools.

The funniest moment travelling was going to China in 2000. We caught the train from Hong Kong, five of us – each carrying about 500 kg worth of luggage. At the Chinese border you had to get off the train, and carry your luggage across. The border police weren't very amused. Kevin's extra luggage consisted of eight tyres.

The Race to the Sky was always an event where the team could relax, and socialise together. We'd take our families along for a bit of quality time together, and all go out to dinner at night. In the summer holidays, the Bourne, Sanderson, and Kitzen families would often get together at Lake Ohakuri, and spend time water-skiing. We got to know Possum better than most people, and got to see the side that the public doesn't see. He was an ordinary bloke who could get ordinary people to do extraordinary things. And above everything, he was my good friend.

RACE TO THE SKY

Sponsors often wonder why I want to keep on winning championships that I've already won. They fail to understand the reason we do it is not for the results, but because we're doing what we want to do, and we've worked damn hard to put together the best team we can in this part of the world. Fortunately, people like Nick Senior and Trevor Amery at Subaru Australia, have been with us long enough to experience the good and the bad. They've felt the same elation when we've won, and the same gut-wrenching disappointment when we've failed to finish. It's these emotions that keep everyone going in rallysport. If you don't feel these, then the effort of the team doesn't mean anything for you. You need passion to generate the motivation for a sponsor to underwrite the million-dollar exercise that is a rally championship-winning campaign. If you don't have passionate people making the funding decisions, then the relationship will only last a short term. With Nick and Trevor, I was very lucky. They were now totally committed to the sport. They'd gotten used to me telling them that we'd need two million bucks to win another Australian championship. Trevor would often quip, "And how much will it cost us to finish second?" But he was only pulling my leg.

Besides, Trevor had tangible evidence that his investment in us was paying a return. In 1995, Subaru Australia sold 8,000 cars for the year, 75 of which were WRX Imprezas – the model most associated with rallying. By 2002, there'd be 27,000 Subarus sold in Australia, including 4000 WRX Imprezas. Our rally campaign was the hub of a successful marketing strategy, and the budget was roughly 20 percent of what Holden invest each year in V8 Supercar racing.

So when I said we'd need a 2000-spec WRC Impreza for the 2001 season, there was instant agreement despite the $1 million cost. What a bloody car. It was just fantastic. Shit, it was fun to drive. It might have looked exactly like my previous WRC Impreza, but it was quite different mechanically. The new car was a bit unreliable at first, as Prodrive and Subaru were still sorting it out, and we had a crap Rally of New Zealand with it. Craig Vincent and I retired with engine problems in my last drive in a WRC Impreza in my home rally. Across the Tasman, however, things couldn't have gone better. With Ed Ordynski concentrating on the Group N class, Neal Bates and I quickly settled into our usual battle for the Australian championship, and this time I held the advantage in terms of the cars we were driving. Neal was driving the same Corolla WRC he'd used the previous season. However, things didn't get off to a great start.

At the first ARC round in Perth, I had an embarrassing half-spin at the opening Friday night super-special stage in Busselton. We sat for what felt like minutes as I struggled to select reverse to get the car back on the track. It took around 20 seconds before I finally found the gear, and Neal began the next day with a 19-second lead. I was determined to overtake him, and it took most of that Saturday to do it. We finally got to the top of the leaderboard that afternoon, only to get caught out by a hole on the inside of a fast corner. It almost ripped the front suspension out of the car. Cody Crocker hit the same hole and broke a control arm. We limped out of the stage and repaired the damage, but it was too late. Neal won Heat One of the championship, while we climbed back up the field, passed Group N winner Ordynski on the way, and finished second.

To keep Neal from winning the round outright the following day would require winning every stage. We went at it like a bull at a gate, Cody hunting down Ordynski with similar determination. We completed a clean sweep of all the stages,

winning Heat Two by one minute and 35 seconds from Neal.
Cody was third, and tied with Ed for the overall Group N honours.
With Neal and I scoring an equal number of stage wins – giving
no chance of a tie-break – there were four cars on the podium!

The see-saw battle between the WRC-spec Subaru and Toyota,
and its near mirror image in the Group N race between Cody and
Ed, made for some spectacular TV, and a large crowd turned up
at the next round in Canberra hoping for a repeat of the Perth
battles. Instead, it was all blue at the front of the field on the first
day. Neal's Corolla dropped a driveshaft, and Cody finished second,
two minutes behind me. Next day Neal's car broke another
driveshaft, as did Ed's Group N Lancer. It was a gift win despite a
suspension problem that morning, although Neal did come back
strongly enough to overtake Cody for second overall.

That Canberra win sort of set the tone for the rest of the
championship. What a bloody car. I felt invincible in it. Like the
others, we'd have our share of problems – a puncture here, a
wrong set-up or tyre choice there. If we did strike trouble, we'd
win by a matter of seconds – if we didn't, the gap to the others
would be measured in minutes. By the sixth round in Melbourne,
we had the opportunity to seal the championship on the first
day by winning Heat One. The brakes started leaking fluid on
one of the stages, but we got it sorted, and came back to win
despite Neal running us close. With the sixth Aussie
championship in the bag, I could relax on the second day, and

just let that hoot of a car rip. We went for imaginary style points instead of fastest times, and started hanging out the tail a bit more than optimum. Despite scrubbing off more speed than we really should have, we still won. Shit, it felt good.

By contrast, the Rally of Australia was a total let-down, although Cody overcame a slipping clutch to finish strongly enough to give Subaru Australia the manufacturers' title in the ARC. We didn't get off to a good start. Engine problems dogged us through testing, and although we thought we'd got on top of them, the motor blew on day two, just when we were putting in a bit of a charge. Still, we were pretty happy with what we achieved in 2001. It wasn't easy, despite the car, and that's the whole point. We overcame plenty of hurdles together as a team, and that's what keeps you coming back. It's not the results that matter, it's the people working together to achieve those results. Everyone made a contribution.

By now, Possum Bourne Motorsport was getting pretty big. Kristine had slipped easily into a permanent role as my P.A. as soon as her kids went to school. We'd started a performance centre as well across the road, complete with all-wheel-drive dyno so we could develop upgrades for Subaru street machines. One of our products was the "Possum Link", new engine management software for turbocharged Subarus that Kevin co-developed with Electro Systems, a Christchurch firm. Launched in 1997, it

became a reasonably strong seller anywhere turbocharged
Subarus were sold. When we got the dyno a couple years later,
it was to develop more "little earners" like that. The aim was to
develop a kit with STi, so that anyone could turn their Impreza
into an affordable Group N rallycar just like that. They could
just get the bits off the shelf, and do it themselves, or ship the
car to Pukekohe, and we'd do it for them. It was hard trying to
keep two businesses running, and drive as well, so I hired Murray
Brown to be general manager.

We were getting prepared for the 2002 season when we got the
news that the Australian Rally Championship would adopt
Group N rules. At first, I thought it was a backward step. The
cars wouldn't be so spectacular, or so fast; and I wondered how
they'd fare on TV. On the other hand, the competition would be
tougher, and I'd have to dig deeper to win. Winning the title in
a Group N car would be a lot harder than the previous six titles,
as strong class runners like Simon Evans, Dean Herridge, Scott
Pedder, and my team-mate Cody were now contenders. However,
it was a sad day when we packed up the WRC car for the last
time, put it in a box, and sent it back to Banbury. I took everyone
out to the Maramarua Forest for one last run. I took the whole
team out and anyone who'd supported us – our sponsors, our
friends, and our families. We burnt up plenty of gas and tyres
over one section of forest road just to celebrate what a fantastic

experience it was to drive that car. The last person to jump in the passenger seat was Kristine. She loved that WRC car almost as much as I did. We both finished the run with tears in our eyes. It was the end of an era.

For those lucky enough to make the grade, moving up from a Group N car to a WRC is considered a steep learning curve. I found it harder going the other way. A Group N rallycar doesn't go, handle, or stop anywhere near as well as the WRC version. It's a harder car to drive from the speed point of view, harder to get going fast all over the stage. There's definitely more things you can do with a WRC to make it work. But life goes on, and Group N had to be our focus now. If we did well enough in the "production" class, maybe we'd compete again at WRC level in the future.

People knew I'd struggle to adapt. Suddenly I was the measure they judged themselves by, rather than the car I drove. They were saying I didn't have a shit show now – which only made me more determined to prove them wrong. It was quite a struggle at first, especially on the suspension front. The options were much more limited in terms of set-up, and it was hard to get the car to settle down. For the whole season, we'd focus most of our development on making the car easier to drive. I'd like to see the Group N rules allow more sophisticated suspension in the future. Not only would it help the cars be more competitive in a WRC rally, it'd help drivers stepping up to the premier class develop more set-up skills.

Was I feeling confident at the start of the first round of the Australian championship in Sydney? Definitely not. Especially as Ed Ordynski, with many seasons of Group N experience behind him, now looked to be in the box seat to win the title. As Mark Stacey clocked in, my plea for help to Rodger took on a new edge. I was about to face one of the biggest challenges of my career, and needed all the assistance I could get. The Harbour City Rally confirmed my worst fears. Ed came out of the blocks hard, and drove brilliantly to win both heats. We retired on both days, our competitiveness wiped out by a string of irritating punctures. Leaving Sydney without scoring points suddenly made our learning curve a lot steeper. It also proved right the pundits who were predicting the end of my title-winning run, and my confidence slipped to an all-time low. It was hard to adapt my driving style to the slower car. I needed to drive smoother and bank away corner speed like it was precious gold, and this was at odds with my usual chuck-it-in-as-hard-as-you-can approach. Our second-generation Impreza was also quite a bit heavier than the first-generation WRX driven by Simon Evans, and it was clear that we'd need more engine development to help overcome the weight handicap.

By the second round in Perth, we'd sorted a few things out. We won the first heat by 11 seconds from Scott Pedder, with Ed finishing third. Scott kept up the pressure all day, and this helped me get the most I could from the car. If you're forced into a situation where you have to go for it, and it all works out, that does wonders for your confidence. The longer the day went on, the more I felt comfortable with the car. By the end of Heat One, I was as confident with it as I had been with the WRC the year before.

Next day, the heavens opened, and the muddy conditions made the Group N Impreza feel heavier than ever. The suspension set-up that had worked so well the day before, now felt wrong for the conditions, and it was really hard work just keeping the car on the road. Simon Evans, in the lighter Impreza, pulled away ahead of us, while Ed and I fought tooth-and-nail over second place. By the final super-special stage at the Nannup Showgrounds, we were tied for runner-up. We then both recorded a time of 31 seconds flat, and took identical points for the heat. I felt totally exhausted by the end of the rally, but there were also feelings of relief. We had some decent points at last, even though I'd never taken so many chances to score them.

The close battle with Ed continued at the next round in Queensland. On the first day, I pipped him for the heat by just three seconds after driving 144 km worth of special stages. The Queensland roads were quite demanding after the smooth gravel of West Australia. On some stages there was long grass growing all over the road, and this made the surface quite slippery. By the final two tarmac stages of the Noosa hillclimb, I had a lead of four seconds, and wondered whether I'd be able to defend it. Ed's a good driver on the tar, while

I definitely prefer a looser surface. However, I drove as smooth and fast as I could, and Ed pulled just one second closer in the Lancer, and had to be content with second.

Next day, Ed rolled out of the second heat on the first stage. I almost got caught out by the same corner as well. It was a long right, and we clipped a bank with the rear of the car. The impact tried to spin us the other way. Fortunately, I gathered up the car, and kept on trucking. It was really hard work on those Queensland back roads, but also bloody enjoyable work. We finished 50 seconds in front of Cody, and felt we were now back in contention for the title. Events where you have to work your arse off all weekend are the ones you enjoy, and remember, the most; and the 2002 Queensland Rally is right up there with my best drives.

Ed made it clear that he wasn't about to give up the title chase at the next round in South Australia. On the first day he beat us all in the state that's home to Mitsubishi Motors Australia, finishing 17 seconds ahead of Mark and I. We struggled to head off Simon Evans for second. We made a wrong tyre choice at the start of the rally, and the Impreza was sliding all over the place. Then, on the eighth special stage of the day, the right-rear propshaft broke just as we took off from the start. So I pressed the diff-lock switch, and put the car into front-wheel-drive for the rest of the stage. We dropped 37 seconds on Ed over those 19 kilometres, but I was happy with that, as I thought I'd lose a lot more time. We replaced the propshaft, and started to charge back up the leaderboard. Going into the final stage at the Wayville Showgrounds, Simon was just ahead of us in second. It started pouring down, turning the horse track to mush. Yet our Impreza carved a graceful, opposite lock slide all the way around it, and we won the stage by four seconds, enough to overtake Simon for second.

In the second heat I knew I'd have to charge right at the beginning of the day to beat Ed. So it was pedal to the metal over the first two stages, and we opened up a nine second lead. It wasn't much of a gap, but it was enough of a margin to defend. Ed would take back another three seconds as the day the progressed, but he finished second in the heat, with Cody third. Our 13 stage wins over the two days were enough to get us declared the overall winners of the South Australian round.

That win on Mitsubishi Australia's home turf must have put huge pressure on Ed. He lasted just four stages of the Rally of Tasmania before crashing out big time. While Ed was carted off to hospital to get treatment for the ribs he broke in a violent argument with a telephone pole, Cody made the most of his misfortune. He won the day by 18 seconds after we chased suspension settings and tyre choices all day. Nothing seemed to work. That night we checked out the 4wd system, and found the centre diff had been on its way out all day. No wonder we couldn't get the car set up.

Next day, the car was perfect, and it was time to pay Cody back. By the final stage, he'd won seven stages of the rally, and I'd won eight. We both recorded a time of one minute two seconds, giving me the overall win courtesy of winning one more stage. What's more, I now had 150 points – 26 more than Ed. After the disastrous start to the championship in Sydney, no one would have predicted I'd be in the points lead going into the final round in Melbourne. But then, Ed's crash had changed the championship. Now, the big threat to my title defence no longer came from our traditional rivals – Mitsubishi – but from within our own team: Cody.

When I finished second to Simon Evans on the first day in Melbourne, Cody still had an outside chance of taking the title. If he won Heat Two, and I didn't finish, we'd be tied for the championship on points. Once again Simon Evans emerged as the fastest man on the second day of the rally, but he was to have rotten luck. His car broke 800 metres from the finish of the final stage, and his retirement handed me the win. I couldn't believe it. I felt sorry for Simon, as he deserved to win that final round, but it still felt bloody good to be the Australian Rally Champion for the seventh time in a row. It wasn't because it was a new record for the history of the sport down under. It was because it'd been so incredibly hard to win. The way the team had come back into contention through the season was awesome. We didn't let the set-backs get us down, and worked hard to overcome the obstacles. There was the getting used to the new car, the punctures in Sydney, and the drive-shaft breakage in South Australia, yet we still won. The sweetest victories are always those you work hardest for. No bastard had given us a chance, which helped our motivation. When somebody tells me I can't do something, that generally means I'll put every effort I can into doing it.

Outside Australia, we had more success in 2002. At the Rally of New Zealand, Mark and I won the Group N class despite a strong entry list of World Group N Championship contenders from Europe. Most drove Mitsubishi Lancers, and after Toshi Arai crashed, and Cody's car broke a gearbox, we were the only Subaru at the leading end of the class. Through most of the rally we battled with the Lancers of Sohlberg and Ligato for the class win, and led them home by 19 seconds. We finished in 13th position overall – one place behind the Group A Impreza of Bruce Herbert, who won the honour of being the first placed Kiwi in the rally. Still, first Group N car home was as good a position as we could hope for with our car in that field. It got me thinking about Group N, and its status within world rallying. The class has strong support in our part of the world, but in Europe, the 1600 cc class is seen as the feeder series for young, talented drivers to make an impact before stepping up to WRC level. Group N has traditionally been "Mitsubishi's championship", as they are the only factory to fully get behind the class. If I could persuade STi that a Group N campaign deserved factory support, it would stop Group N being a "one-horse race", and the extra competition for the "production" car title might attract the interest of other manufacturers. Rallying needed to resolve its regional differences in the secondary classes at WRC rounds. In the Asia-Pacific region, Group N was more important as it had three Asian manufacturers – Mitsubishi, Subaru, and Proton – producing cars that could be readily modified into Group N rallycars. In Europe, the 1600s ruled thanks to the influence of European manufacturers who saw the class as a good marketing tool for hot hatchbacks. For me, Group N cars made more sense as the second tier to the championship, as the dominant Mitsubishis and Subarus were 4wd vehicles with strong mechanical ties to WRC cars. Getting a factory-supported team of Subarus together for an assault on the World Group N championship in 2003 would up the ante for the class, and hopefully raise its global profile.

If I'd hoped that a good result in the class at the 2002 Rally of Australia would help persuade STi to support such a campaign, the car failed me. On the Special Stage 8, the Impreza ground to a halt with a blown engine. However, winning the Japanese round of the Asia-Pacific Rally Championship at Hokkaido late in 2002 won more kudos for our team, and an even warmer reception at STi when we came to discuss the 2003 season. We also competed in a tarmac round of the Japanese championship and pulled off a 1-2 Subaru finish with Toshi Arai. We were back in world rallying at last, and signed up to a two-car assault on the Production World Rally Championship – one for me, and one for Toshi. Possum Bourne Motorsport would supply most of the parts and crew, working in partnership with Subaru Yogima (a.k.a. Subaru International Motor Sports) and STi. With lots of New Zealanders like Tony Sircombe, Toshi's co-driver, included in the team, I told Pirelli, our tyre sponsor, that we were "the Kiwi Mafia" of the production class.

The Italians would later tell me that our input had made the production class better to watch than the WRC cars. With Peugeot spending the most money to dominate the premier class, they thought the PWRC class now offered the best opportunity for a close battle. And that's exactly how the season began to play out. My strategy called for a decent result in the first round in Sweden, followed by class wins at the second round in New Zealand, and hopefully the third in Argentina – a place I'd already competed in before.

Sweden, however, was a totally new experience, and I'd never driven competitively on so much ice and snow before. At least Mark and I had the warmest place to work of anyone in the team. During the second day of testing, the temperature dropped to minus 28 degrees. Although the crew wore insulated snowsuits and woolly hats, they still froze their balls off.

Sweden was total culture shock in terms of rally conditions, and one of the local Karstad newspapers renamed me "Bambi Bourne" after doing a feature on the driver who'd travelled the furthest to the rally. Stig Blomqvist gave me a few driving tips which were very helpful, allowing me to be a bit more aggressive on the narrow tyres, and snow-ploughed roads. He showed me how to use the snow banks to take corners at higher speeds, or to slow down if I got into one too fast. Usually you come off a corner with some opposite lock on the steering. Stig showed me how to turn the wheel the other way just before the car hit a snow bank so that just the rear of the car hits the bank. There were a few interesting moments during testing while trying Stig's tips. On one corner, we misjudged the braking point, and the car smacked into the snow bank hard at around 130 km/h. Fortunately, it just bounced back onto the road, and we carried on. It gave me a better idea of how hard I could go.

My big worry in Sweden was the studded tyres we were using. The production rules allowed only 30 tyres per rally, and if we started breaking the studs off the tyres, the traction went with them. We started the event cautiously, and it took time to get settled in. After the second leg, I was just about to order the crew to change the centre diff as the car was under-steering everywhere. Then I asked Toshi and Stig about the handling of their Imprezas and they reported the same reluctance to turn. Turned out the centre diff was fine – it was just the effects of the conditions that were causing our car to handle that way. As we got more used to the ice and snow, and once we'd tuned the engine for more power, our position in the PWRC class began to improve. Before we adjusted the intercooler water spray, we noticed Toshi's car was hitting 200 km/h on the straights while ours would top out at 182 km/h. We'd eventually finish fifth in the class on the road, 7.8 seconds behind Martin Rowe. Toshi and Tony had the class won until two stages from the finish. They retired with an engine problem, handing the line honours to a Polish driver who was later to be disqualified for having an illegal flywheel fitted to his Mitsubishi. I was mildly disappointed with fourth place in the class, but it was a dream result compared with how we'd go in New Zealand. There, we lasted just five stages before the engine packed a sad. Toshi won the class, which was some compensation for the heart-break in Sweden.

The PWRC campaign placed a lot of pressure on the team, as we still had to fulfil our commitment to Subaru Australia to defend the Australian championship as well. This created a bit of a logistical nightmare for Murray and Kristine. The 2002-spec car used in Sweden was shipped back for the first round of the Aussie series in Perth, while the service truck would stay there for later European rounds of the championship. The 2003-spec car used in New Zealand would go to Cyprus to meet up with the service truck used in Sweden, while yet another car would stay in Australia to take care of business there. The ARC round in Western Australia didn't go well from a personal point of view. We retired with engine problems, but fortunately Cody won both heats for the team, and team-mate Dean Herridge would have finished second overall had his gearbox not expired on the second day.

With a mediocre result in Sweden, followed by mechanical disasters in Perth and the Rally of New Zealand, the 2003 season wasn't shaping up as well as we'd planned. I was really looking forward to blowing some of the stress away at the Silverstone Race to the Sky hillclimb in Wanaka that Easter. I first went there in 1998 for the first Race to the Sky, and loved the event straight away. It was an absolute blast – a hillclimb that's more a mountain climb, rising 5000 feet over 15 kilometres of rough gravel road, with 139 corners to complete, including nine hairpins. A time of eight minutes and 30 seconds was the current record and I aimed to blow it away. We had a special 600-horsepower Subaru Impreza that the boys had created out of a former WRC-spec Subaru complete with active suspension. As I'd won the event in 2001 with a 400 bhp Impreza – essentially a Group A rally car without its restrictor – I was keen to find out what an extra 200 bhp would do for us. Up against us were the usual suspects – "Monster" Tajima in the factory-developed 900 bhp twin-turbo V6-powered 4wd Suzuki Aerio, and Rod Millen – the first New Zealander to win the Asia-Pacific rally championship – with his awesome V8 Toyota Tundra pick-up. I'd broken Monster's three-time winning streak in 2001, and Rod had won the following year. The Race to the Sky was the down under equivalent of Pike's Peak – and attracted a similar number of factory-developed prototypes. If I won there again in a Subaru, I'd have liked to take the same car to Pikes Peak, painted black and with a big silver fern on it – just like the livery of most New Zealand international sports teams.

Far from the pressure of a championship series, the Race to the Sky was also a family event. Rod would be bringing out his family from California, and Monster his new bride from Japan. For Peg and I, it was a chance for the kids to get involved in my sport, and when I won in 2001, Taylor and Spencer joined me on the podium to celebrate. That the memory lived on in their heads was clear from the 47th birthday cards they gave me in April – Spencer's had a picture of the course he had drawn, winding its way up the Pisa mountain range. This would be more than just another race – it was to be quality family time together, a chance to enjoy ourselves in a spectacular part of the country before I flew to Canberra for the next round of the Australian Championship. Race to the Sky organiser Grant Aitken was happy to make some accommodation at the Snow Farm at the top of the hillclimb available to us. In winter months, the Snow Farm is a top-secret winter testing ground for car and tyre manufacturers to test their prototypes in ice and snow. Developer John Lee invested more money in the facilities with the bookings he received over the years, and we were happy to stay there together with Grant's blessing. It was all the incentive I needed to compete in his event – it was always such good fun, and definitely my favourite event in the world.

AFTERWORD

APRIL 18TH 2003 – GOOD FRIDAY

That day we woke up to a beautiful crisp morning. Snow was all around the Snow Farm, where Possum, our family, and our team were staying for the Race to the Sky 2003 event. All the vehicles out front were covered with snow. People were outside trying to clean it off their cars and make them warm enough to travel down the mountain in. Everyone was on a high. This event was going to be a cracker.

Over breakfast, Possum and his crew went over what had to be done that day. First, there was the job of completing the set-up of our service tent. Several of the team had arrived days earlier to get everything ready for Possum's arrival. Second was getting the car ready for testing that morning, around the RallySprint track at the bottom of the hill. Then the car would have to be loaded on to a truck with other competitor vehicles, and taken to Queenstown for the "Rally Show". The cars would be on display and the drivers on hand for interviews and autographs, and generally in the public eye as the lead up to the Race to the Sky. After that, the last job would be getting the car back to the mountain base where the service crew would prepare it for qualifying the next day. It was going to be a big day.

Possum left with most of the crew early that morning to go down the mountain to the service park. He left as he always did: hyped up, excited, and ready to take part in his favourite event and get going. During breakfast he had enjoyed watching his children play in the snow as he "murdered" his last cup of tea (a favourite saying of his). As the team loaded up the van we were using, Possum came back in one last time to kiss and cuddle the three kids in his usual rush-out-the-door fashion. His smile to me and quick peck was as normal. I could tell that he was fired up in anticipation of his day.

After waiting for several supplies to take to the team, I loaded up all the children, including their cousins, and headed down to join Possum. The chatter amongst the children was constant as they all pretended to be Possum driving down the mountain. It was so beautiful to drive out of the snow and down the mountain to the service park. Possum's comments the night before kept coming back to me. "Wow!", he said. " Monster and Rod are going to be bloody hard to beat... the road is so flat and wide...it's like driving on tarmac." Then he finished with his usual, "Grrr..." – a way of his wanting to fight back, even though the event hadn't even started.

By the time we reached our service tent, the boys were well and truly tuning and making last minute touches to the car. Possum was tinkering away, making sure all the right signage was on the car correctly, and adding stickers. He always made sure that his sponsors were looked after properly. It had to be perfect.

As the sun finally made a showing, and we were all warming up, Possum changed into his overalls at the back of the tent. The kids were all running around him getting excited, then they would disappear when the boys revved the engine, as it was quite loud.

And then Possum was off. It was natural for almost everyone in that pit area to be drawn to the bank incline – where most spectators watch the event from – to see Possum testing his car. It was spectacular to watch. I always get a tingle in my spine when I see him in action. He makes it look so good, and so easy. If there was any thought in my head while I was watching him, it was "He's got 'em this time!"

The car was "grouse", another of Possum's favourite words. After several runs around the bottom track, he got out of the car and waved to a few of his mechanics to come down and make some small changes. And then he was off again. It was awesome to watch. Never did I dream that this was the last time we would ever see Possum in action. This was Possum's year. Everything we had worked so hard and for so long to achieve was happening. And this event was just the icing on the cake because it was so much fun.

Our kids and their cousins sat on the incline watching Possum, and then, with their Matchbox toy cars, they pretended they were him going around and around.

After he finished the testing and brought the car back into the tent, Possum disappeared for about 10 minutes. Later I was to find out that it was during this time his last interview was being carried out. I will never forget him bounding back with that spring in his step and that smile on his face. He announced he had forgotten to bring his Number One "work clothes" – his nice gear, publicity shirt and nice trousers – down from the Snow Farm, so that he could go on to the Rally Show in Queenstown. He asked if anyone was using the Forester, and went to jump in to go back up to the Snow Farm just to get changed. He asked me if I wanted to go with him, or wait at the tent. Before I could respond, Spencer went to get in the car with him. That was always the case with Spencer – where Dad goes, Spencer goes. But at the very last second, Spencer saw that his brother Taylor and his cousins were heading on into Queenstown to go riding on the luge, and changed his mind. After all, Poss and I wouldn't be far behind them.

Since Jazlin was with me, I decided to sit in the sun and wait for Possum to return. He wouldn't be long. His last words to me were, "I'll be right back Babe!"

Peggy Bourne

PETER - OUR POSSUM

Peg and Ray of Mercer, had a little baby boy,

A second son for them to love, and bring them loads of joy,

Sadly, his older brother was taken home again,

So Peter, small, then unaware, helped to ease their pain.

He then grew up the older son, of a family of whom we're proud,

But he was fated to be someone, to stand out in a crowd.

It soon became clear to Peter, and he thought it so neat,

That he liked things mechanical, especially if it had a seat.

He learned to drive the tractor, and finally the car,

And he thought then, perhaps this skill would maybe take him far.

So in his Mum's old Humber, out driving just one day,

He came upon a possum, a crossing on his way.

He tried so hard to miss it, he really did his best!

But crashed his mother's car, instead, to miss this little pest!

Well history was made that day, a legend it was born,

For we now had "OUR POSSUM", the world would see his form.

In Woodhill northern forest, he starts at forty-eight,

He was a new unknown, and the day would seal his fate.

For he came in, at number three, the drive it was a winner,

And from now on, the Rally scene was going to see a grinner.

In the "Spirit of South Auckland", he raced with local pride,

And sometimes though it didn't work, we all know how much he tried.

Now people in Japan had watched the progress of this man,

And Subaru thought, if anyone could, this man surely can.

So now he was professional, the star of Subaru,

He drove their car, and flew the flag, to them he was so true.

The rest they say is history, he rallied far and wide,

And in Kenya, his greatest win, Peggy, his lovely bride.

She asked if he could dance as well as he drove a car,

He must have, for they became the happiest by far.

Now Possum was in his element, a happy married chap,

For his little Peg, and family, that's where his life was at,

For home was where his heart was, while he was away,

And landing back in Auckland, really made his day.

For although the world is very good, there is no place like home,

Because the only contact, while away, is talking on the phone.

For family time together, as a family means so much,

And whenever Possum got there, it was done without a fuss.

But he was also dedicated, to his workers, and his fans,

And they were always uppermost, in any of his plans.

For nothing was a problem, any reasonable request,

For anyone, big or small, he always gave his best.

At the end of any rally, he'd sign his autograph,

And although he might be weary, he did it with a laugh,

To Possum, people mattered, it's what makes the world go round.

And in his life of giving, that is what he found.

He never looked back in anger, at things that might have been,

Just a shrug of those broad shoulders, his passion just stayed keen.

Cause Possum, you were special, you'll never be replaced,

And the world is going to miss your lovely smiling face.

You've left the world a better place, because of what you've done,

A family that's so proud of you, as a father, brother, son.

So now you've gone to rally, in the race track in the sky,

The hardest thing for most of us is we really don't know why.

One day perhaps we'll understand, why it was you that had to go,

But just right now, it does not make sense, just a sad and tragic blow.

So God, wrap your arms around him, and his family left down here,

Give them strength to carry on, for the loss they have to bear.

And all of us, here today, to grieve and to mourn,

And say farewell, to the one we loved, our one and only

Possum Bourne

Written by Possum's Uncle, Graham Clendon and read by him at Possum's Prizegiving, at Pukekohe, on Tuesday May 6th 2003.

TAYLOR BOURNE'S EULOGY

Dad, you were a great man.

I will miss you.

I hope you are having a great time

in heaven with Stefan's dad, Rodger.

I love you, Dad. I miss your smile.

Mum, Jazlin, and Spencer are also sad.

Everyone is sad about you, Dad.

Dad, we all want you to know that

we really miss you.

We really want you to come back.

I really, really, really love you, Dad.

You are in my heart, Daddy.

I love you infinity.

From

Taylor

Written by Possum's 8-year-old son Taylor, and read by him at Possum's Prizegiving, at Pukekohe, on Tuesday May 6th 2003.